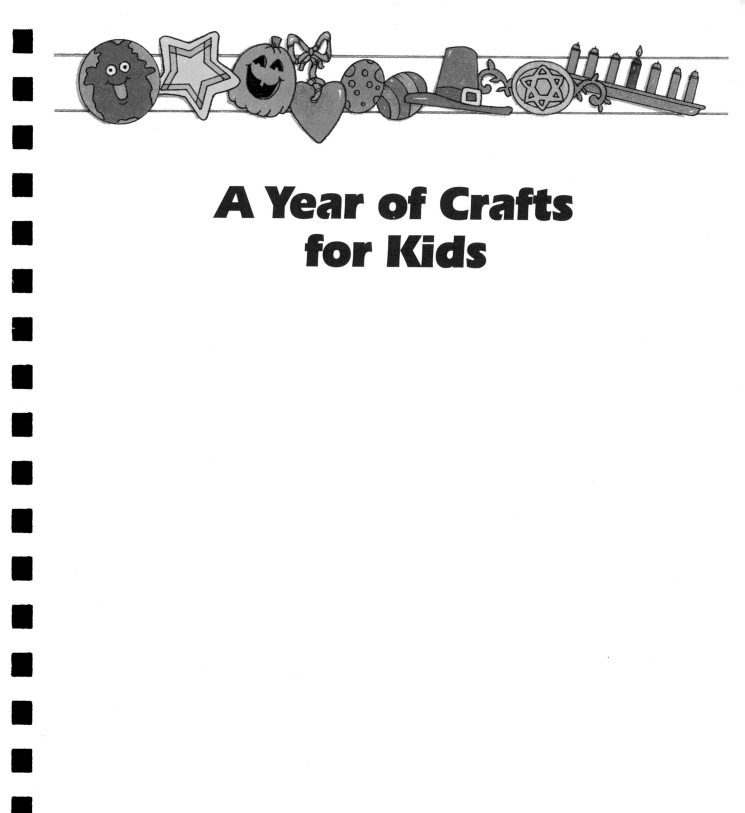

A Year of Crafts
for Kids

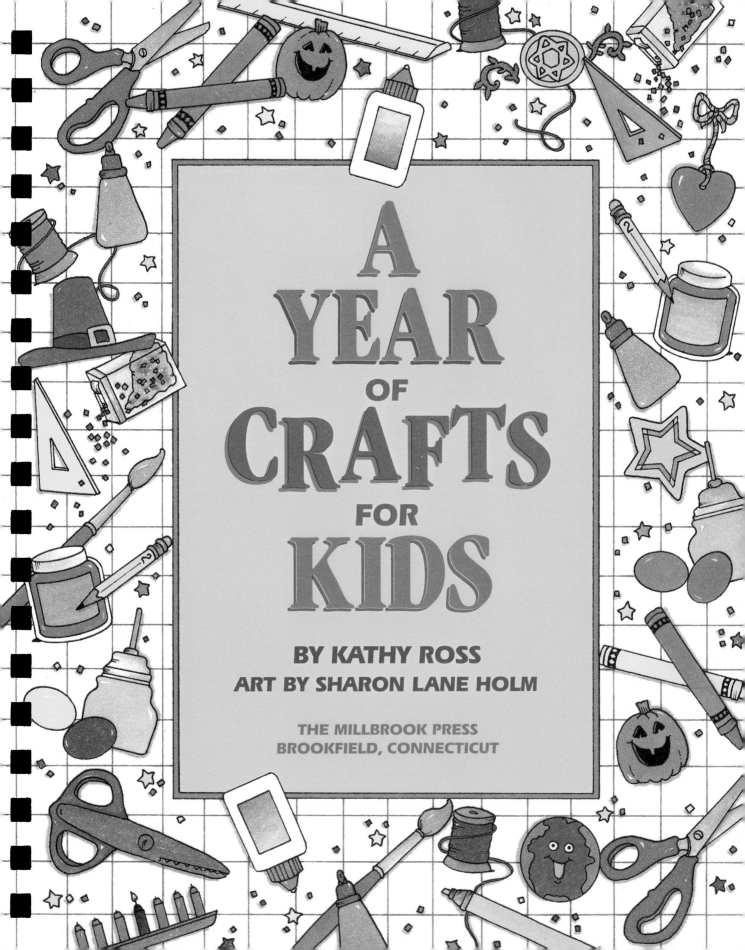

A YEAR OF CRAFTS FOR KIDS

BY KATHY ROSS
ART BY SHARON LANE HOLM

THE MILLBROOK PRESS
BROOKFIELD, CONNECTICUT

To Judie Mills,
the best art director ever!
K.R. and S.L.H.

ISBN 0-7613-1002-9

Published by The Millbrook Press, Inc.
2 Old New Milford Road, Brookfield, Connecticut 06804

The crafts are selected from *Crafts for Valentine's Day, Crafts for Easter,
Every Day Is Earth Day, Crafts for Halloween, Crafts for Thanksgiving, Crafts
for Hanukkah, Crafts for Christmas*, and *Crafts for Kwanzaa* by Kathy Ross.
The collection has also been published under the title
The Best Holiday Crafts Ever!

Contents

Happy Valentine's Day!

Valentine's Day is celebrated on February 14. It is a time for telling family and friends—and sometimes someone you wish you were friends with—how much you care about them. People do this by sending valentines—paper cards and hearts with a valentine message written on them.

No one is really sure how Valentine's Day actually got started. Some believe it originated with a priest named Valentine who lived a long time ago. It is believed that he secretly married young lovers who had been forbidden to marry by the laws of the time. Another story tells of a man named Valentine who was sent to prison for his religious beliefs. It is said that the children of his town loved him very much and sent notes and flowers to him in prison.

Today we celebrate Valentine's Day by exchanging cards, candy, and flowers. It is not a legal holiday on which schools, banks, and post offices are closed, but it is just the right time for telling people you care about them.

Wallpaper Envelopes

Make your valentine mail extra special by sending paper hearts in these beautiful envelopes.

Here is what you need:

pretty pieces of wallpaper from old wallpaper books

envelope of the size you want your envelopes to be

scissors

valentine or flower stickers

white glue

pencil

Here is what you do:

1. Carefully unglue the seams of your envelope and flatten it out to use as a pattern. Steam helps to loosen the glue, so leaving the envelope in the bathroom while you shower should make it come apart quite easily.

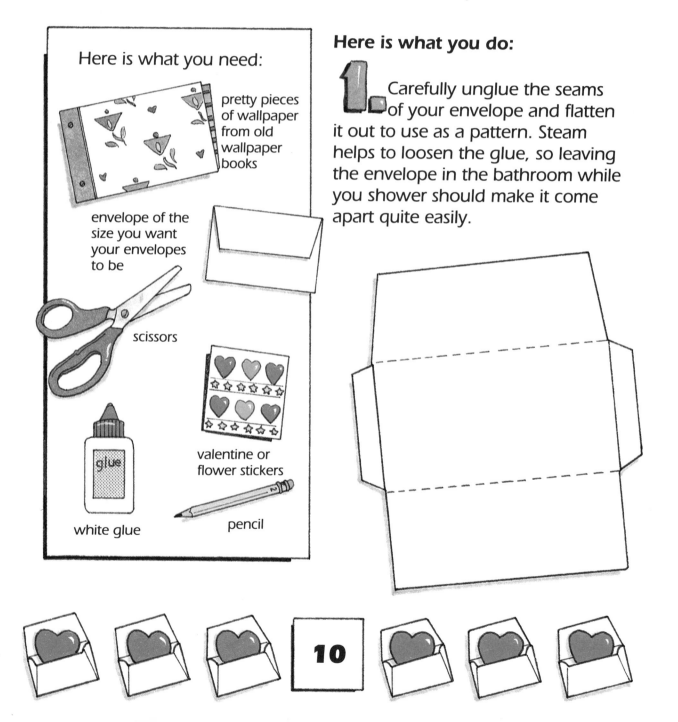

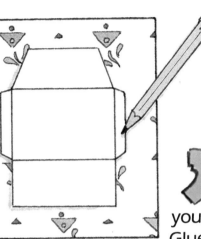

2. Choose a pretty piece of wallpaper and trace around the pattern on the paper. Try to center the envelope so that whatever picture is on the wallpaper will appear in a pleasing arrangement on the envelope.

3. Carefully cut the envelope out and fold it at all the places that your pattern envelope was folded. Glue the folds in place, leaving the top open.

4. These envelopes are perfect for paper hearts with a Valentine's Day message. Just slip the hearts in the top and seal the envelopes shut with a pretty sticker.

If you don't have any wallpaper, you can use heavyweight gift wrap instead.

Heart Mouse

Whoever gets to pull on the tail of this little heart mouse will get a surprise.

Here is what you need:

red and pink construction paper

scissors

stapler

black marker

white glue

flat lollipop

Here is what you do:

1. Fold a piece of red construction paper and cut a half heart about 3 1/2 inches (9 centimeters) high on the fold. Leave the heart folded to form the body of the mouse.

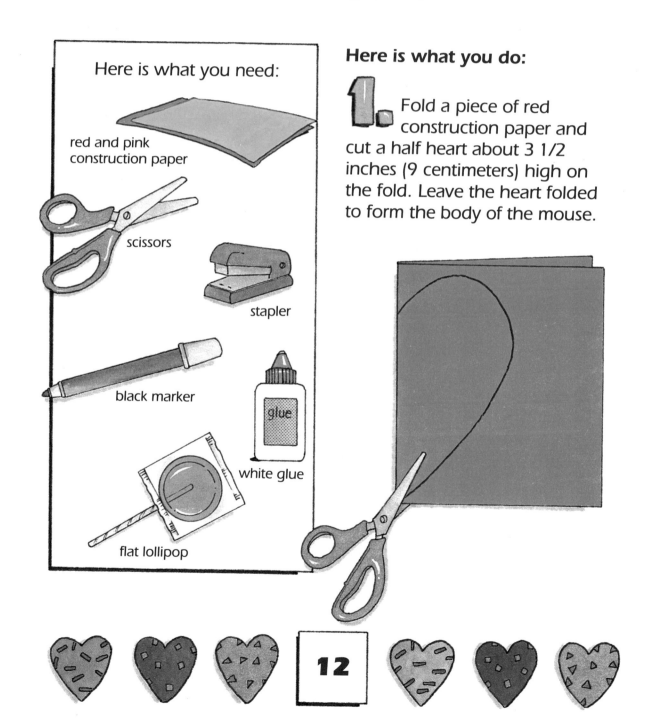

2. Cut a smaller heart from the red paper for the head of the mouse. Cut a slit about halfway up from the point of the heart. Wrap the two sides of the slit around to form a cone nose and staple them in place. Use a black marker to draw eyes and a nose. Staple the head to the pointed end of the heart body. Staple the rounded end of the body so that it forms a pocket.

3. Cut a tiny heart from red paper. Write PULL on the heart and glue it to the stick end of the lollipop. Cut a heart from pink paper to cover the lollipop. Write your valentine message on this heart and glue it over the wrapper. Tuck the lollipop into the body of the mouse so that the stick end is sticking out to form the tail of the mouse.

Happy Valentine's Day! love Greg

Pull

Make a mouse for each of your friends.

Pull

Pull

Valentine Crown

Make a friend feel like royalty with this crown.

Here is what you need:

paper plate

red poster paint

paintbrush

scissors

white glue

newspaper

conversation hearts candy

Here is what you do:

1. Cut a slit across the middle of the plate, starting about 1 inch (2.5 centimeters) inside the outer rim and stopping about an inch inside the rim on the opposite side of the plate. Starting in the center of the plate, cut four more slits to create six pie-shaped sections. Fold the sections up to make a crown.

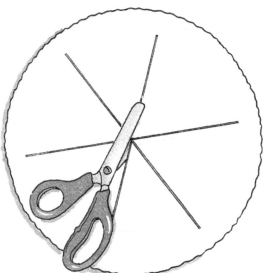

2. Paint the plate red on both sides and let it dry.

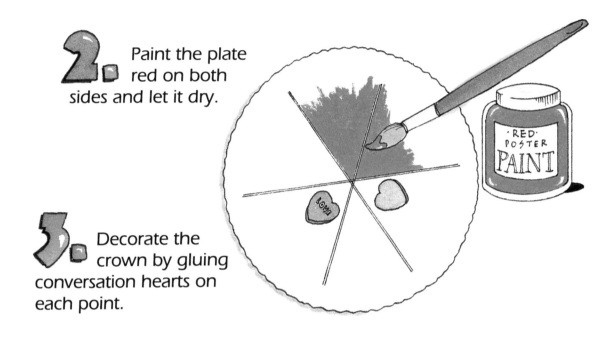

3. Decorate the crown by gluing conversation hearts on each point.

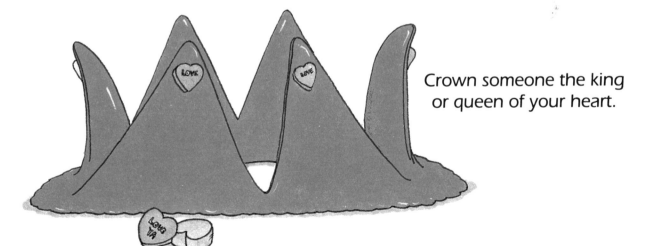

Crown someone the king or queen of your heart.

15

Card Man Favors

Here is what you need:

old deck of playing cards

red pipe cleaners

red construction paper

black marker

stapler

round ball lollipop for each favor

Here is what you do:

1. For each favor you will need a heart playing card for the front and an extra card to use as the back. Only the back of this card will show.

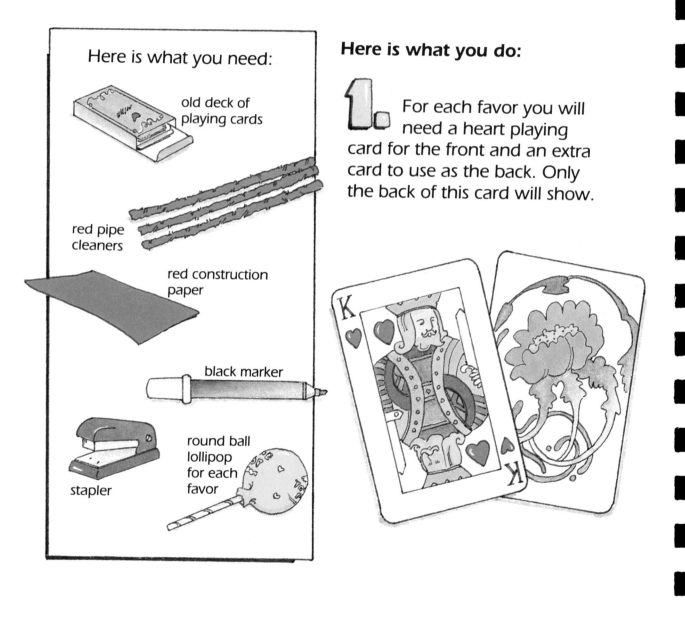

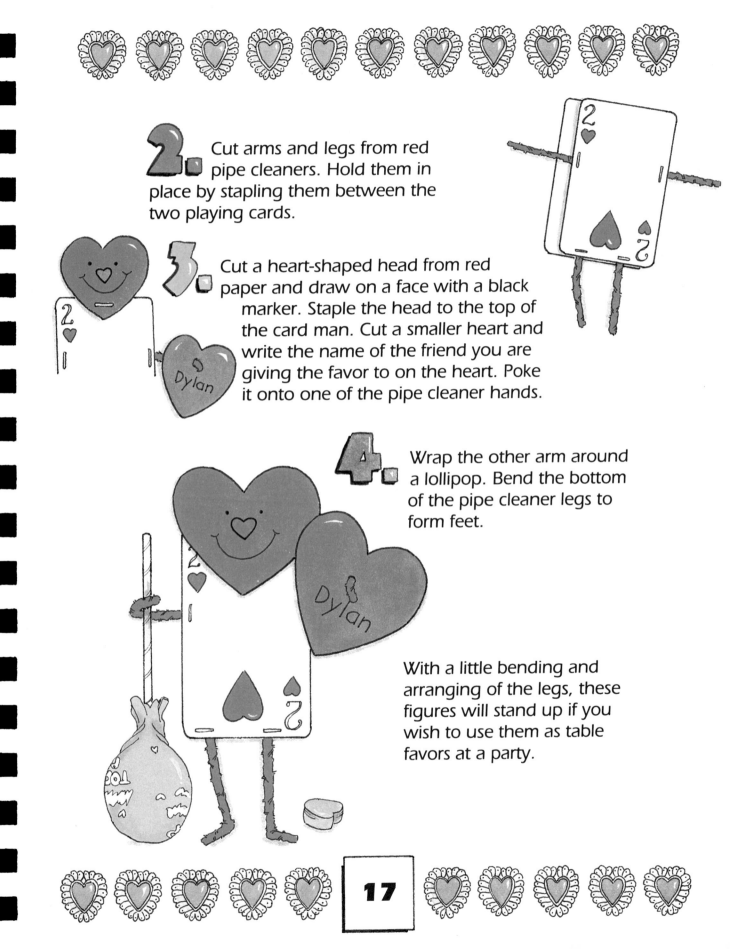

2. Cut arms and legs from red pipe cleaners. Hold them in place by stapling them between the two playing cards.

3. Cut a heart-shaped head from red paper and draw on a face with a black marker. Staple the head to the top of the card man. Cut a smaller heart and write the name of the friend you are giving the favor to on the heart. Poke it onto one of the pipe cleaner hands.

4. Wrap the other arm around a lollipop. Bend the bottom of the pipe cleaner legs to form feet.

With a little bending and arranging of the legs, these figures will stand up if you wish to use them as table favors at a party.

Castle Mail Holder

Here is what you need:

square tissue box

four paper towel tubes

red poster paint

paintbrush

white glue

black, red, and pink construction paper

black pipe cleaner

scissors

newspaper to work on

Here is what you do:

1. Trim the four paper towel tubes so that they are 3 inches (8 centimeters) taller than the tissue box. Cut eight evenly spaced, 1-inch (2.5-centimeter) slits around the top of each tube. Fold in every other tab around each tube to form the castle turrets.

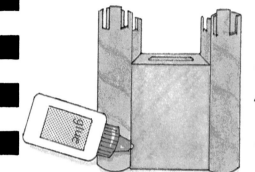

2. Glue a tube on each corner of the box to make the castle. After the glue has dried, paint the castle red.

3. Cut a door and windows for the castle from black paper and glue them on. Cut hearts from red and pink paper to decorate the castle. Cut a pink triangle flag and write your name on it. Cut a red heart to glue on next to your name then glue the flag to one end of a black pipe cleaner. Glue the flag on one side of the castle.

Keep this castle mail holder on your desk all year to stash your special notes and letters in.

Dove
Table Decoration

Here is what you need:

half of a Styrofoam ball small enough to fit inside the lid

lid from a small jar

white glue

red glitter

five white Styrofoam packing worms

blue ballpoint pen

six black pipe cleaners

yellow, white, and pink construction paper

scissors

newspaper to work on

Here is what you do:

1. Glue the flat side of the half Styrofoam ball into the jar lid. Cover the sides of the jar lid and the ball with white glue and sprinkle with red glitter to completely cover.

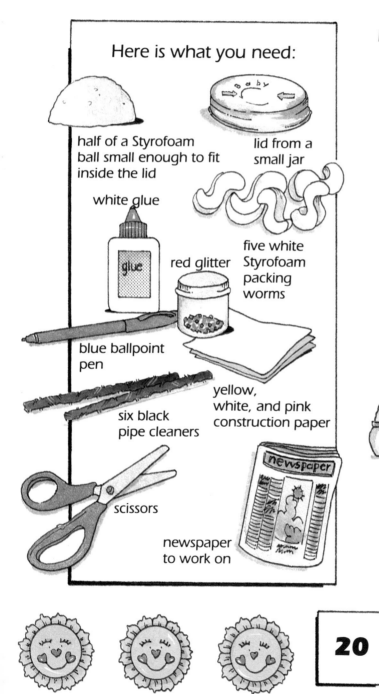

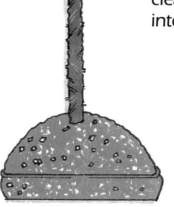

2. Stick one packing worm on the end of each pipe cleaner and poke the other ends into the Styrofoam ball.

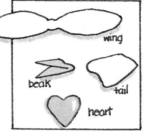

3. To make each dove, cut wings and a tail feather from white paper and a beak from yellow paper. Glue them in place on each dove. Cut tiny hearts from pink paper to glue in each bird's mouth. Add eyes with a ballpoint pen.

These valentine doves will look very sweet flying around on the table of someone special to you.

21

Valentine Card Garland

Here is a great way to use old valentines and decorate your room at the same time.

Here is what you need:

red yarn

scissors

red and pink construction paper

old valentine cards

cellophane tape

hole punch

Here is what you do:

1. Cut hearts from red and pink paper. Make them about the same size as the cards you will be using. Punch two holes in the top of each paper heart and each card.

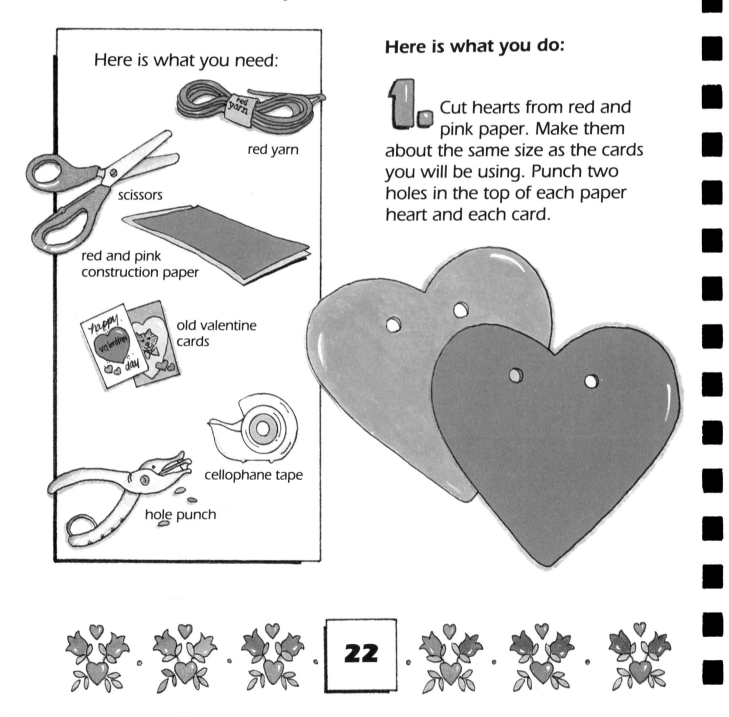

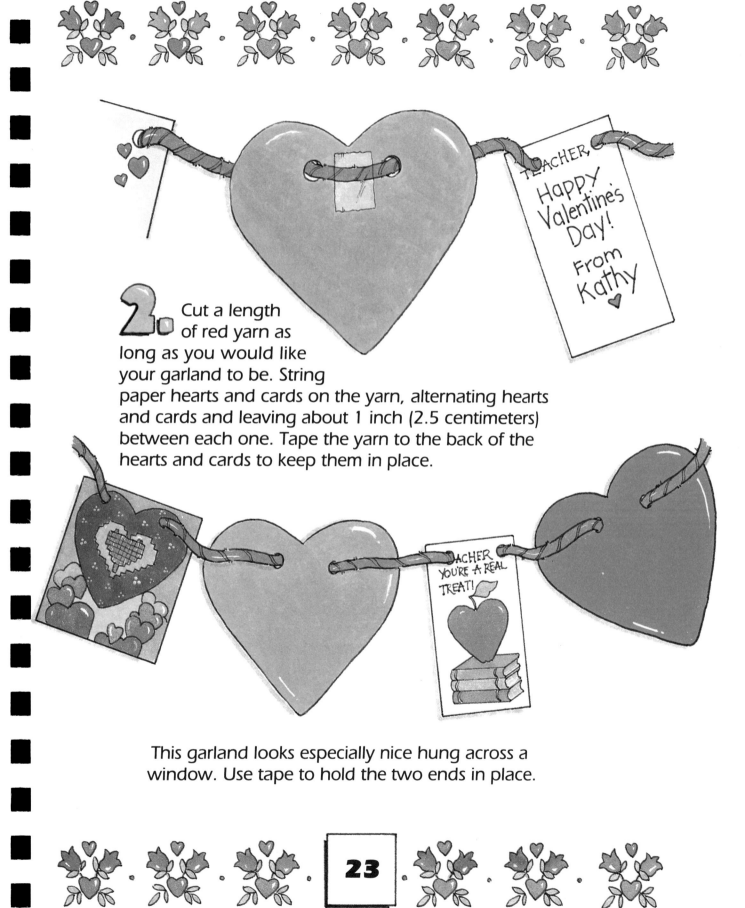

2. Cut a length of red yarn as long as you would like your garland to be. String paper hearts and cards on the yarn, alternating hearts and cards and leaving about 1 inch (2.5 centimeters) between each one. Tape the yarn to the back of the hearts and cards to keep them in place.

TEACHER, Happy Valentine's Day! From Kathy

TEACHER YOU'RE A REAL TREAT!

This garland looks especially nice hung across a window. Use tape to hold the two ends in place.

Heart Man

Make this giant heart to keep you company this February.

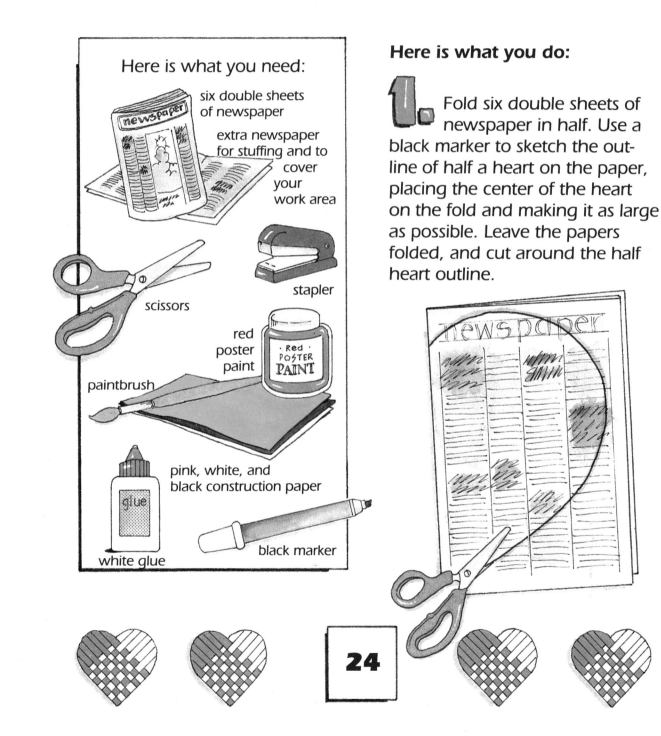

Here is what you need:

six double sheets of newspaper

extra newspaper for stuffing and to cover your work area

scissors

stapler

red poster paint

paintbrush

pink, white, and black construction paper

white glue

black marker

Here is what you do:

1. Fold six double sheets of newspaper in half. Use a black marker to sketch the outline of half a heart on the paper, placing the center of the heart on the fold and making it as large as possible. Leave the papers folded, and cut around the half heart outline.

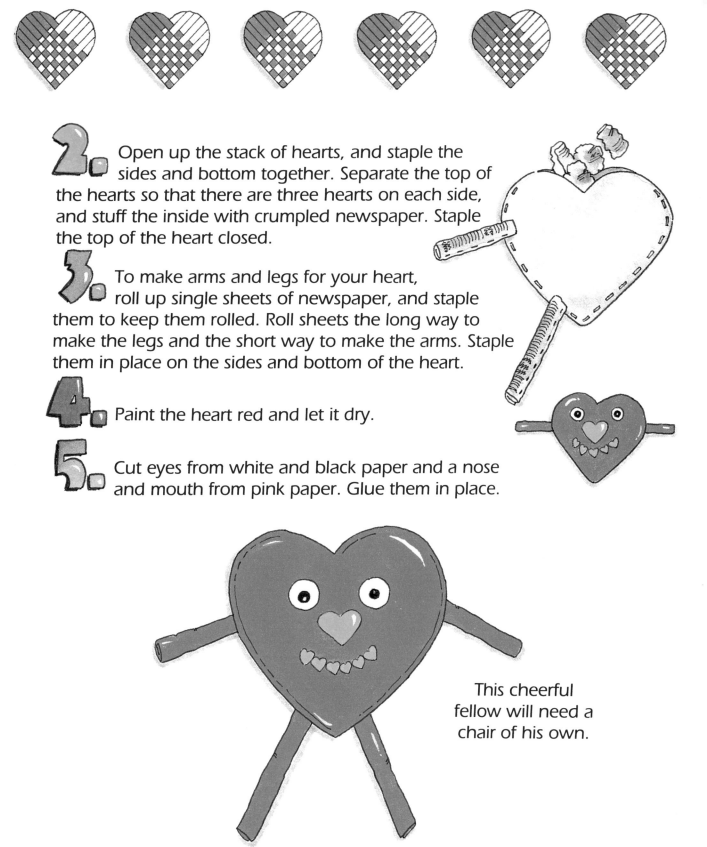

2. Open up the stack of hearts, and staple the sides and bottom together. Separate the top of the hearts so that there are three hearts on each side, and stuff the inside with crumpled newspaper. Staple the top of the heart closed.

3. To make arms and legs for your heart, roll up single sheets of newspaper, and staple them to keep them rolled. Roll sheets the long way to make the legs and the short way to make the arms. Staple them in place on the sides and bottom of the heart.

4. Paint the heart red and let it dry.

5. Cut eyes from white and black paper and a nose and mouth from pink paper. Glue them in place.

This cheerful fellow will need a chair of his own.

Valentine Guest Soaps

Here is what you need:

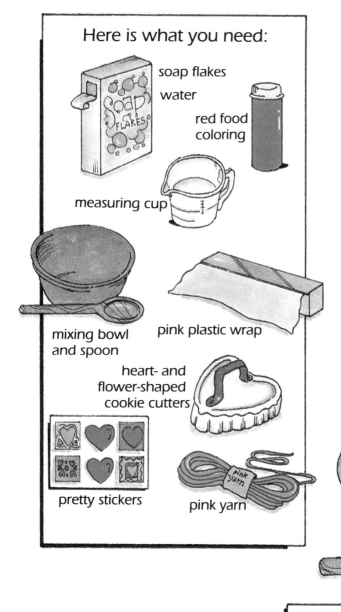

soap flakes

water

red food coloring

measuring cup

mixing bowl and spoon

pink plastic wrap

heart- and flower-shaped cookie cutters

pretty stickers

pink yarn

Here is what you do:

1. Put two cups of soap flakes into a mixing bowl. Squeeze a few drops of red food coloring into 1/4 cup of water, and add it to the soap flakes. Mix until the soap is evenly colored. If the mixture sticks to your fingers, add a little more soap. If it is too dry and crumbly, add just a tiny bit more water.

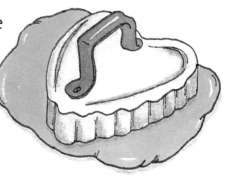

2. Press small amounts of the mixture on a clean counter, and cut heart and flower shapes with the cookie cutters. Put the shapes on a plate, and let them dry and harden for two days.

3. Decorate each soap with a pretty sticker. Wrap three or four soaps in a square of pink plastic wrap, and tie with pink yarn.

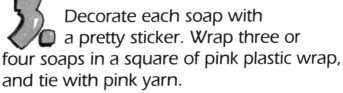

If you don't have any stickers to decorate your guest soaps, use little pictures of hearts and flowers cut from old greeting cards. Just attach them with a tiny dot of white glue.

Heart Magnets

Here is what you need:

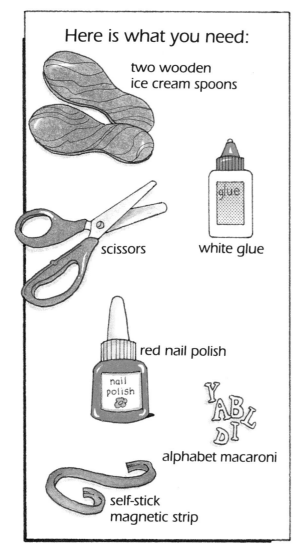

two wooden ice cream spoons

scissors

white glue

red nail polish

alphabet macaroni

self-stick magnetic strip

Here is what you do:

1. Cut 1 inch (2.5 centimeters) off the wide end of each spoon for a big heart and 1 inch off the handle end of each spoon to make a small heart.

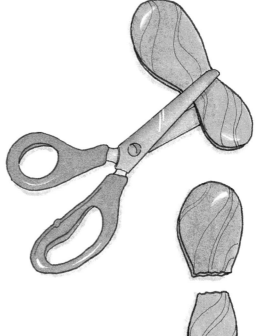

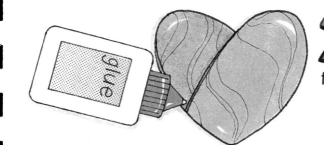

2. Place the pieces across each other and glue in place to form the hearts.

3. When the hearts have dried, glue a piece of magnetic strip on the back of each heart. Paint both hearts with red nail polish, and let them dry again.

If you would like to write a name or message on your hearts you can do this by gluing on tiny macaroni letters.

Valentine Scrapbook

Make a special scrapbook to keep your valentines in.
It is fun to look back the next year and find favorite
old cards from favorite old friends.

Here is what you need:

four brown
grocery bags

newspaper

red tissue or
wrapping paper

matching
ribbon

white glue

glue

old greeting
cards

scissors

Here is what you do:

1. Cut each of the bags along the seam. Then cut the bottom out so that you have four long pieces of brown paper. Stack the four pieces and fold them in the middle to form a book.

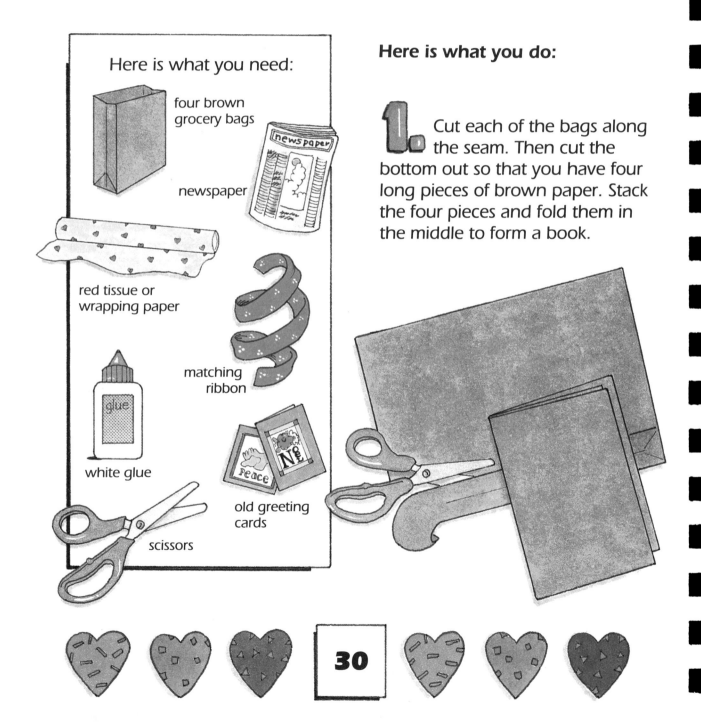

2. Make a heart pattern from newspaper to exactly fit over the front of the book. Then trim the book into the shape of a heart. Be very careful to leave a part of the folded side of the book uncut so that it holds together.

3. Use the newspaper pattern to cut a pretty cover for the book from wrapping paper. Glue the wrapping paper heart to the front of your book.

4. String ribbon through the center of the scrapbook and tie the ends in a bow at the front of the book. Cut the letters of your name from old greeting cards and glue them on the front of the book.

Fill your book with pretty valentines.

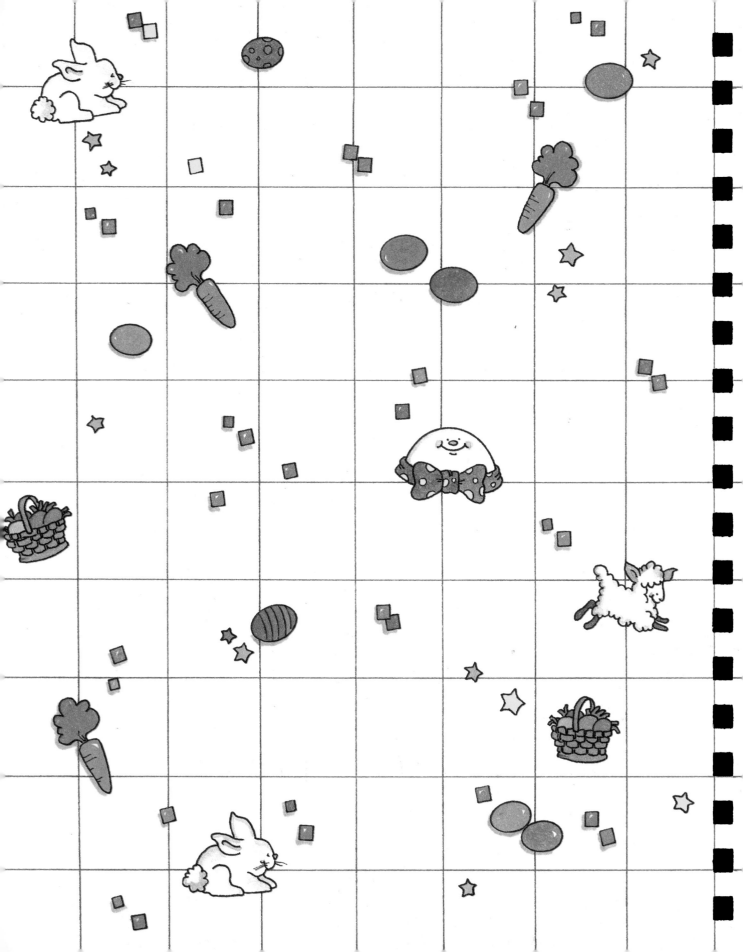

Happy Easter!

Easter always falls on a Sunday in March or April, but it can be on a different date each year. It is celebrated on the first Sunday after the first full moon following the first day of spring, the twenty-first of March.

For Christians, Easter is the joyous time when they remember that Jesus Christ came back to life. Many people who are not Christian also take part in traditional Easter activities. Children expect a visit from the Easter Bunny, who hides decorated eggs for them to find. Children may wake up and discover a basket filled with candy, brightly colored jelly beans, or chocolate eggs.

Easter can be a celebration of springtime, when animals are born and flowers appear again after the cold winter months. Pink tulips and yellow daffodils, baby chicks and lambs, new outfits and bright hats—Easter celebrates new life.

Stuffed Bunny Friend

Everybody loves the Easter Bunny!
Here is a bunny for you to make.

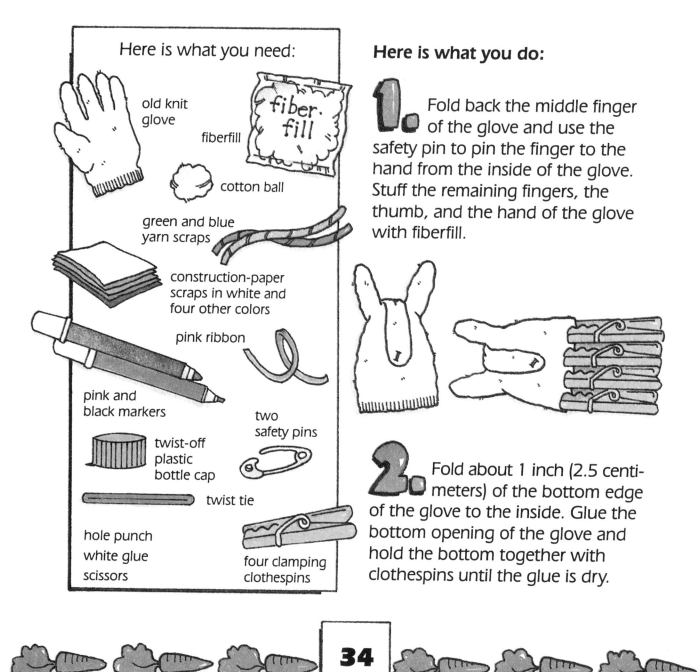

Here is what you need:

old knit glove

fiberfill

fiber fill

cotton ball

green and blue yarn scraps

construction-paper scraps in white and four other colors

pink ribbon

pink and black markers

twist-off plastic bottle cap

two safety pins

twist tie

hole punch
white glue
scissors

four clamping clothespins

Here is what you do:

1. Fold back the middle finger of the glove and use the safety pin to pin the finger to the hand from the inside of the glove. Stuff the remaining fingers, the thumb, and the hand of the glove with fiberfill.

2. Fold about 1 inch (2.5 centimeters) of the bottom edge of the glove to the inside. Glue the bottom opening of the glove and hold the bottom together with clothespins until the glue is dry.

3. Make a basket for the bunny by covering the sides of the bottle cap with pink ribbon. Fill the cap half full with glue. To form a handle, stick the two ends of the twist tie into the glue on each side of the cap. Fill the cap with snips of green yarn. Squeeze more glue on top of the yarn and glue in some eggs punched from papers of different colors. Let the basket dry.

4. Pull the thumb and little finger of the glove forward to form the bunny's arms. Slide the basket over the little finger and safety-pin the thumb and finger together from behind so that the pin doesn't show. Slide the basket over the area where the thumb and little finger join.

5. Tie a pink bow just above the folded arms to define the bunny's neck. Cut paper circles for eyes and put dots in the centers with a marker. Glue them on. Make whiskers by forming a knot in the middle of two pieces of blue yarn and unraveling the ends. Glue the whiskers below the eyes. Glue a cotton-ball tail on the back of the bunny at the tip of the folded-down finger. If the glove you used is a light color, color the center of the ears pink with a marker.

You can also hang the basket on a long piece of ribbon to make a very pretty necklace.

Necktie Bunny Puppet

Old neckties make great puppets.

Here is what you need:

two old neckties

two safety pins

cotton ball

scraps of black, white, and pink construction paper

yarn

scissors

white glue

Here is what you do:

1. Cut across the wide end of one of the ties about 14 inches (35.5 centimeters) above the point. This will be the body of the bunny puppet.

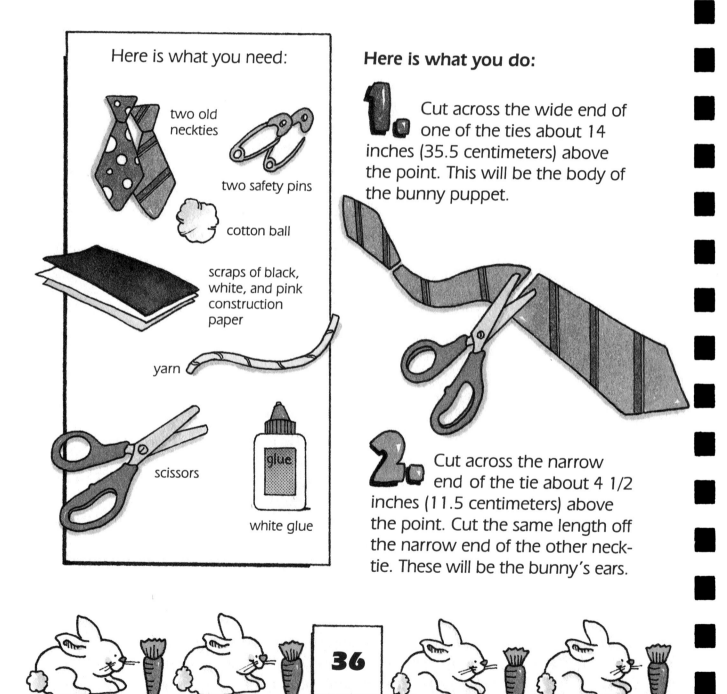

2. Cut across the narrow end of the tie about 4 1/2 inches (11.5 centimeters) above the point. Cut the same length off the narrow end of the other necktie. These will be the bunny's ears.

3. Cut a heart-shaped nose from pink paper. To form whiskers, glue two pieces of yarn to the point of the wide part of the tie. Glue the nose over the middle of the whiskers. Cut two eyes from the black and white paper and glue them above the nose.

4. About 2 inches (5 centimeters) above each eye, cut a small slit. The slits should be just long enough so that the straight ends of the ears, if slightly bunched up, will fit into them. Pin the ears to the body with safety pins, hiding the pins in the folds of the ears.

5. Glue a cotton-ball tail to the body of the bunny and let the glue dry.

To work the puppet, slip your hand between the fabric and lining of the necktie all the way to the point. Fold the head down. The bunny's ears will stand up and allow you to make many different expressions. Hold your bunny tight! Don't let him hop away!

Wallpaper Easter Basket

This pretty little basket is so easy to make you could give one to each of your friends.

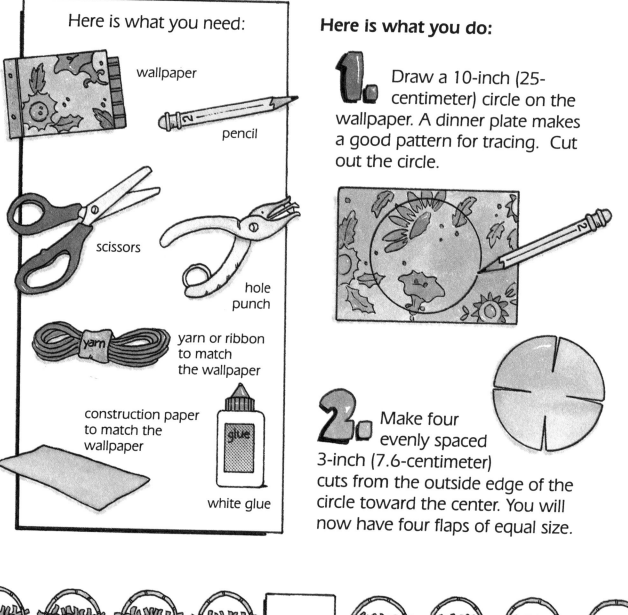

Here is what you need:

wallpaper

pencil

scissors

hole punch

yarn or ribbon to match the wallpaper

construction paper to match the wallpaper

white glue

Here is what you do:

1. Draw a 10-inch (25-centimeter) circle on the wallpaper. A dinner plate makes a good pattern for tracing. Cut out the circle.

2. Make four evenly spaced 3-inch (7.6-centimeter) cuts from the outside edge of the circle toward the center. You will now have four flaps of equal size.

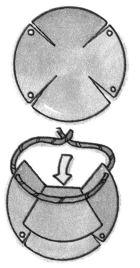

3. Punch two holes, about 1/2 inch (1.25 centimeters) from the edges of two flaps that are across from each other.

4. Cut two pieces of yarn 6 inches (15 centimeters) long. String one piece of yarn through the two holes directly across from each other on opposite flaps. Pull the two flaps together, with the yarn around the outside of the flap between them. Tie the yarn in a bow. Punch two holes and string the other strand of yarn through the flaps on the other side in the same way and pull the circle up into a basket.

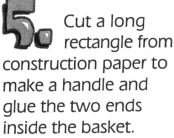

5. Cut a long rectangle from construction paper to make a handle and glue the two ends inside the basket.

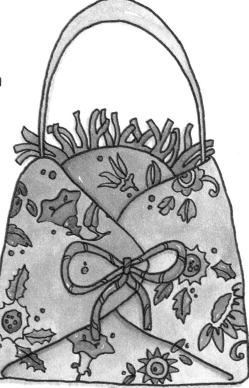

Fill the basket with Easter grass and some special Easter goodies.

Easter Basket
Party Hat

This is an Easter basket to wear on your head!

Here is what you need:

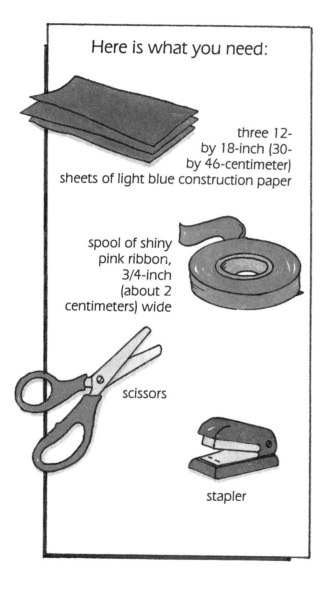

three 12-by 18-inch (30-by 46-centimeter) sheets of light blue construction paper

spool of shiny pink ribbon, 3/4-inch (about 2 centimeters) wide

scissors

stapler

Here is what you do:

1. Fold two sheets of the construction paper in half lengthwise. Staple the ends of the two sheets together to make a band of paper long enough to fit snugly around your head. Be sure the ends overlap slightly and trim off any extra paper.

2. Now fold the band of paper in half lengthwise again and cut 4-inch-long (10-centimeter-long) slits about 1 inch

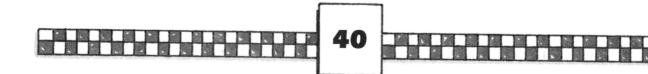

(2.5 centimeters) apart all the way along the band. Do not cut through the folded edge of the paper.

3. Unfold the band and weave three rows of ribbon through the band to make it look like a basket. Staple the ends of the ribbon to hold them in place. Fold the top of the basket over the ribbon about 1 1/2 inches (4 centimeters) and staple it in place to give the basket a neat top edge. Staple the ends of the woven band together to complete the hat.

4. Cut a strip of blue construction paper to make a handle. Cover it with a strip of pink ribbon and staple the ribbon in place. Make a bow from the ribbon and staple it to the handle.

Staple the ends of the handle to the inside of the basket hat.

Don't let a mixed-up bunny put any eggs in this basket!

Basket Full of Easter Friends

Did something in your Easter basket wiggle?

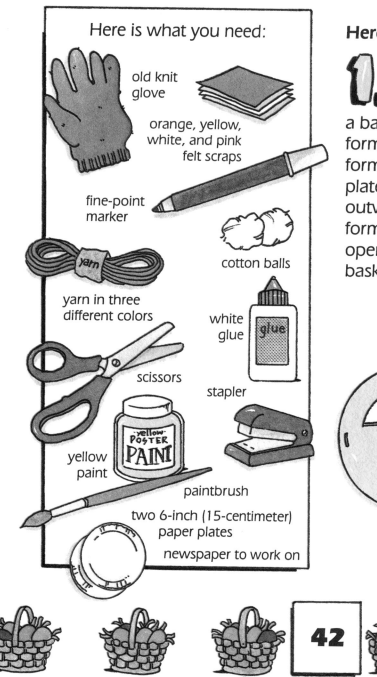

Here is what you need:

old knit glove

orange, yellow, white, and pink felt scraps

fine-point marker

yarn in three different colors

cotton balls

white glue

scissors

stapler

yellow paint

paintbrush

two 6-inch (15-centimeter) paper plates

newspaper to work on

Here is what you do:

1. Cut out half of the center of each plate. This makes a basket shape. The uncut half forms the basket, and the cut half forms the handle. Place the two plates together, bottoms facing outward, and staple the sides to form a basket. Leave the bottom open. Paint both sides of the basket yellow and let it dry.

2. Stuff a cotton ball into each finger of the glove. Tie a piece of yarn in a bow under each cotton ball to hold it in place. This makes a little head at the end of each finger.

3. Turn the fingers into rabbits, chicks, and ducks by cutting eyes, ears, and beaks from bits of felt and gluing them on the heads. Use yarn knotted in the middle and frayed on the ends to make whiskers for the rabbits. Let the glue dry before trying out the puppets.

Put your hand in the glove. Slide the glove into the basket so that the Easter friends are peeking over the basket rim. Can you think of a name for each of your five new animal friends?

43

Three-Envelope Easter Chick

This Easter chick has a surprise inside.

Here is what you need:

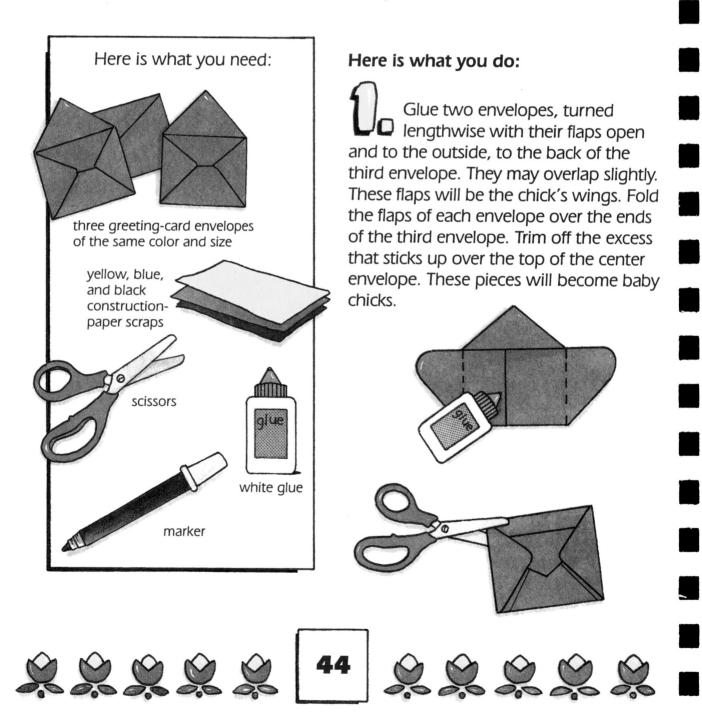

three greeting-card envelopes of the same color and size

yellow, blue, and black construction-paper scraps

scissors

glue

white glue

marker

Here is what you do:

1. Glue two envelopes, turned lengthwise with their flaps open and to the outside, to the back of the third envelope. They may overlap slightly. These flaps will be the chick's wings. Fold the flaps of each envelope over the ends of the third envelope. Trim off the excess that sticks up over the top of the center envelope. These pieces will become baby chicks.

2. Unfold the two wings. Cut eyes and a beak from construction-paper scraps and glue them on the flap of the middle envelope to form a face. Glue the eyes so that the wings will cover them when the wings are closed.

3. Cut beaks and eyes from paper scraps and glue them on the flaps of the two extra pieces to make faces for the baby chicks. Write an Easter message on the bodies of the chicks and then tuck them into the middle envelope. Fold the head of the large chick over the babies, then fold the wings over the face.

If you used white envelopes for this project, color the chicks with crayons or markers.

Fluffy Pinecone Chick

Did that pinecone just "peep?"

Here is what you need:

large, fat pinecone

pencil

yellow paint

fiberfill

paintbrush

white, blue, orange, and yellow felt scraps

green construction paper

Easter grass

white glue

newspaper to work on

scissors

Here is what you do:

1. Paint the pinecone yellow and let it dry.

2. Wrap the pinecone in a thin layer of fiberfill, using a pencil to poke the fluff between the scales of the pinecone.

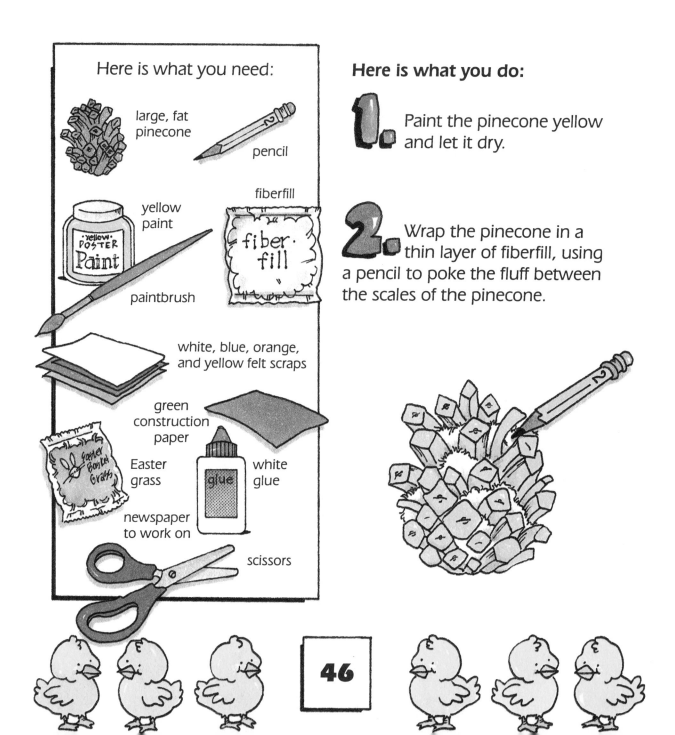

 Cut wings, a beak, and eyes from felt scraps and glue them on the pinecone body.

Cut a 4-inch (10-centimeter) circle out of green construction paper. Glue Easter grass on top of the circle. Then glue the pinecone chick to the middle of the grass.

This little chick makes a very nice table decoration.

Tennis Ball Chick Puppet

If you drop this little chick, it just might bounce away!

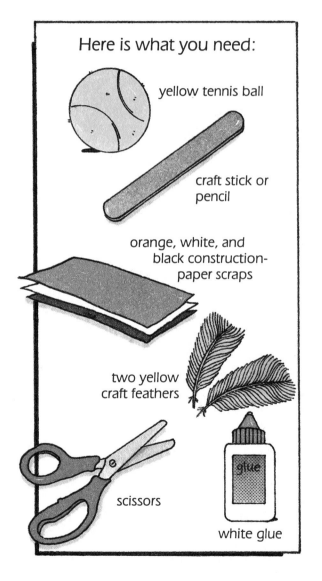

Here is what you need:

yellow tennis ball

craft stick or pencil

orange, white, and black construction-paper scraps

two yellow craft feathers

scissors

white glue

Here is what you do:

1. Ask a grown-up to cut a 2-inch (5-centimeter) slit in the tennis ball with a sharp knife.

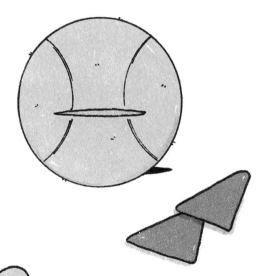

2. Cut two triangle-shaped pieces for the chick's beak from orange paper. Rub glue onto the top and bottom edges of the

slit in the ball. Glue the edges of the triangles to the slit to form the top and bottom of the beak. Slide the craft stick or pencil between the top and bottom triangles and leave it there until the glue has dried so that the triangles are not glued shut.

3. Cut eyes from black and white paper scraps and glue them in place above the beak. Glue two craft feathers to the back of the chick to make a tail. Let the glue dry before using the puppet.

To make the chick's mouth move, just squeeze the ball on each side of the beak. This chick can be used as a party favor, too. Fill it with tiny toys and wrapped candy.

Spring Lamb

Make this lamb to decorate your room for spring.

Here is what you need:

two identical flat rectangular Styrofoam trays

Styrofoam packing worms

masking tape

black construction paper

white hole-reinforcement ring

thin pink ribbon

jingle bell

white glue

scissors

Here is what you do:

1. Cut a head, legs, and a tail for the lamb from black construction paper. Cover the bottom of one Styrofoam tray with masking tape. Glue the head, legs, and tail and ribbon for a hanger to the tape. Cover the bottom of the other tray with tape. Cover the tape on both trays with glue. Glue the trays together.

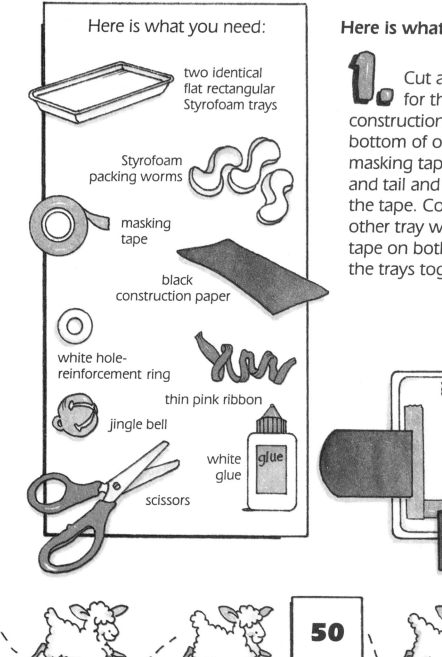

2. Stick the white hole-reinforcement ring on the head for an eye and glue on an ear cut from black paper. String the jingle bell on the pink ribbon and tie it in a bow around the lamb's neck.

3. Cover the front tray with masking tape, then cover the tape with glue. Stick Styrofoam packing worms all over the tray to give the lamb a woolly coat.

Hang this lamb up quickly! He might follow you to school one day!

Handprint Lamb Easter Card

Turn your hand into a lamb to make this special Easter card.

Here is what you need:

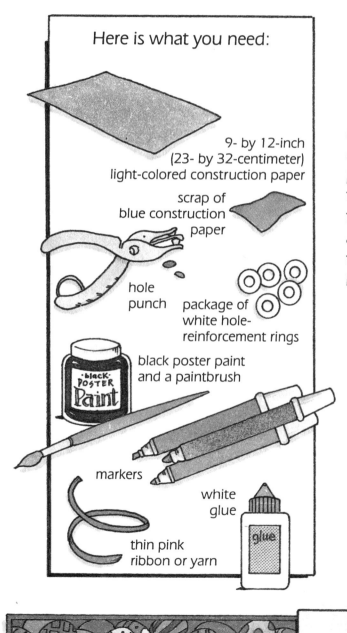

9- by 12-inch
(23- by 32-centimeter)
light-colored construction paper

scrap of
blue construction
paper

hole
punch

package of
white hole-
reinforcement rings

black poster paint
and a paintbrush

markers

white
glue

thin pink
ribbon or yarn

Here is what you do:

1. Fold the construction paper in half to form a 6- by 9-inch (15- by 23-centimeter) card. Paint your palm black with the poster paint. Make a handprint on the front of the card with your fingers and thumb spread apart and pointing toward the bottom of the card. Let the handprint dry before you continue.

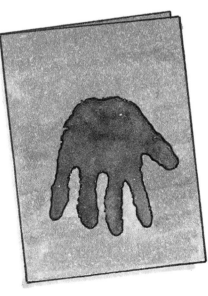

 Cover the hand part of the handprint with the hole-reinforcement rings to make the lamb's woolly coat. The four fingers will be the lamb's legs, and the thumb will be the head.

Use the hole punch to make an eye for the lamb from blue paper. Make a dot in the middle of the eye with a marker and glue the eye to the thumb of the handprint. Glue a pink ribbon bow to the neck of the lamb.

Use markers to add grass, flowers, and a sun. Inside the card, write "Happy Easter from your little lamb" and sign your name.

People you love will enjoy receiving cards made from your handprint.

Designer Easter Outfit

This project lets you design the Easter outfit of your dreams.

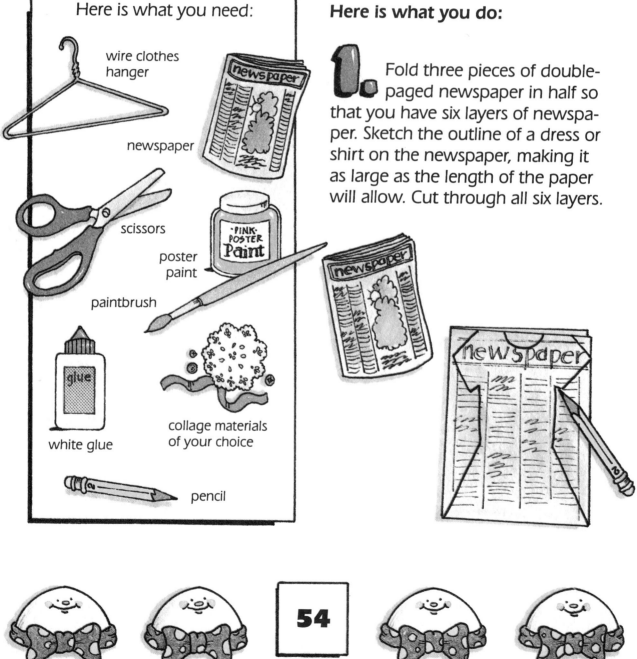

Here is what you need:

- wire clothes hanger
- newspaper
- scissors
- poster paint
- paintbrush
- white glue
- collage materials of your choice
- pencil

Here is what you do:

1. Fold three pieces of double-paged newspaper in half so that you have six layers of newspaper. Sketch the outline of a dress or shirt on the newspaper, making it as large as the length of the paper will allow. Cut through all six layers.

2. Slip a wire hanger between the layers of the outfit at the shoulders so that three layers of newspaper are in front of the hanger and three layers are in back. Squeeze some glue between each layer of newspaper so that the layers of the outfit will stay together.

3. Paint your outfit with one or more colors, being careful not to get paint on the hanger. Decorate your designer original with doilies, sequins, lace, ribbon, feathers, stickers, buttons, or fabric scraps.

Hang your creation up for all to admire.

Puzzle Pieces Easter Wreath

Wreaths aren't just for Christmas anymore!

Here is what you need:

4 cups of old jigsaw-puzzle pieces

white glue

green food coloring

pretty artificial flowers

yellow yarn

9-inch (23-centimeter) paper plate

large mixing bowl

measuring cup

spoon

plastic wrap

hole punch

scissors

Here is what you do:

1. Mix four drops of green food coloring with a cup of white glue. Mix the green glue with all the puzzle pieces in a large bowl. If the mixture seems too drippy, add more puzzle pieces. Stir until the pieces are evenly coated with glue.

2. Cut the center out of a paper plate to form a wreath shape. Punch a hole in the edge of the rim and tie a piece of yarn through it to make a hanger.

3. Set the rim on a piece of plastic wrap on a flat surface where the wreath will be able to dry for several days without being moved. Pile spoonfuls of the puzzle-piece mixture around the rim to form a three-dimensional wreath. You may not need to use all of the mixture. Add or subtract pieces until the wreath looks right to you.

4. When the wreath has dried completely, you can decorate it by gluing on some artificial flowers.

What an unusual wreath!

Celebrate Earth Day!

Earth Day is celebrated on April 22 each year. The first Earth Day was held in 1970 and was celebrated by schools and communities. Special programs informed people of the problems that our planet was facing.

Today Earth Day is celebrated with both education and action. Many people use Earth Day as a time to clean up public places and to plant trees and flowers. It is important to remember that the kinds of things we can do to help keep our planet healthy are things that need to be done all year. That is why the Earth Day motto is "Make Every Day Earth Day."

We need to recycle things so we stop creating so much trash. We need to stop wasting our natural resources, and we need to protect the living space of our vanishing wild animals. We need to stop polluting our air, land, and water and to work hard to clean up those places that are already polluted. Earth Day is a good time to learn about the many things we can do to help Earth be a healthy place for all living things.

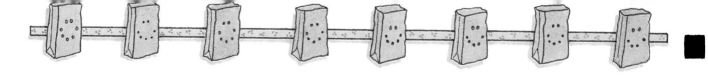

Trash Monster

We need to keep our land clean.

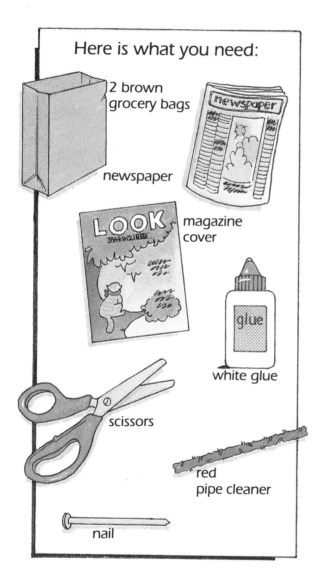

Here is what you need:

2 brown grocery bags

newspaper

magazine cover

white glue

scissors

red pipe cleaner

nail

Here is what you do:

1. Cut a large oval hole out of the bottom of a grocery bag. Open a second grocery bag and slide the first bag inside it so that the bottom with the hole is at the top. The hole is the monster's mouth.

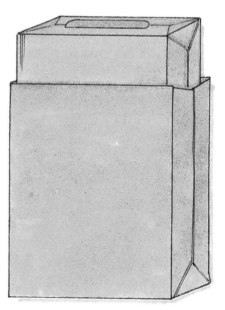

2. Crumple newspaper into balls and glue them above the mouth for eyes. Cut sharp teeth from an old magazine cover and glue them around the inside of the mouth.

3. Cut letters from newspaper ads to spell out "trash monster" and glue them on the front of the bag.

4. Poke holes through the top and back side of the trash monster with a nail, and string a pipe cleaner through. Twist the two ends together to make a handle.

Take your trash monster for a walk and feed it trash you find along the way.

Seedling Necklace

A fun way to watch a seed sprout is to carry
it with you on a necklace.

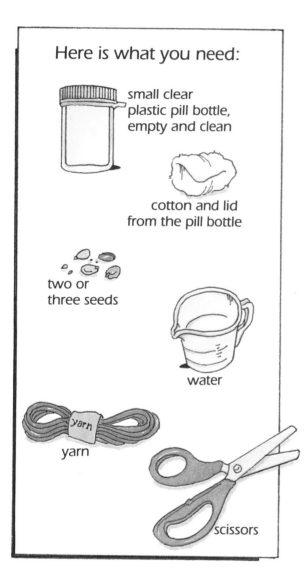

Here is what you need:

small clear
plastic pill bottle,
empty and clean

cotton and lid
from the pill bottle

two or
three seeds

water

yarn

scissors

Here is what you do:

1. Moisten the cotton
saved from the bottle
and squeeze it out. Put the
wet cotton inside the bottle.
Slip two or three seeds between the cotton and the
wall of the bottle and put
on the lid.

2. Tie a piece of yarn around the lid then tie the two ends together to form a necklace.

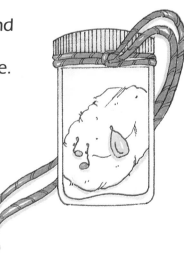

Wear your necklace until your seeds have sprouted. Then plant them in a flowerpot or in your garden.

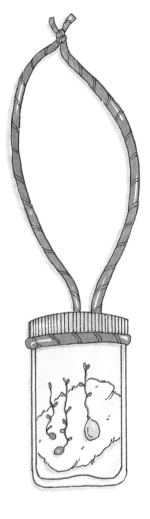

Anna's Seeds

Bag Saver

Don't throw plastic bags away. Use this box to save them so you can use them again and again.

Here is what you need:

- large tissue box
- brown poster paint
- paintbrush
- newspaper to work on
- 5 small green pom-poms
- hole punch
- white glue
- scrap of yellow paper
- 2 small wiggle eyes

Here is what you do:

1. Stand the box on one end. Paint the sides and top brown, like the trunk of a tree. It will probably need two coats.

2. Glue five small pom-poms in a row on the top of your box, to look like a caterpillar. Glue two small wiggle eyes to the first pom-pom.

3. Punch four holes out of yellow paper and glue them on the back of the caterpillar.

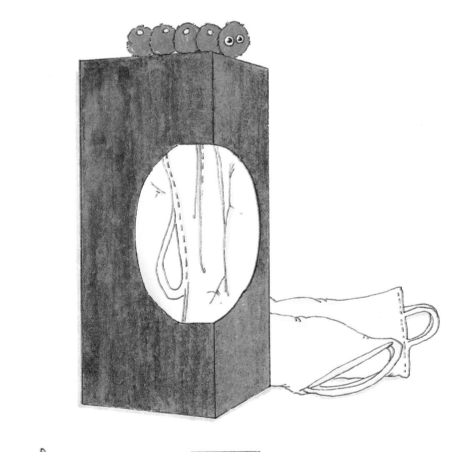

Puzzle Tree

Here's a fun way to recycle an old jigsaw
puzzle that has some missing pieces.

Here is what you need:

yellow and brown
construction paper

old jigsaw puzzle pieces

scissors

white glue

Here is what you do:

1. Cut a tree shape from
the brown construction
paper. Glue the tree on the
yellow paper.

2. Glue the puzzle pieces on the tree for leaves. If your puzzle pieces have lots of red, orange, and brown colors on them you can make an autumn tree and glue some of the pieces at the base of the tree, to make leaves on the ground. Pink pieces mixed in with light green pieces make pretty spring trees. Green pieces are just right for summer trees.

If your puzzle pieces are not the right color for the tree you want to make, just turn them over and paint them the colors you want your leaves to be.

Recycled Wind Sock

We need clean, fresh air to breathe.

Here is what you need:

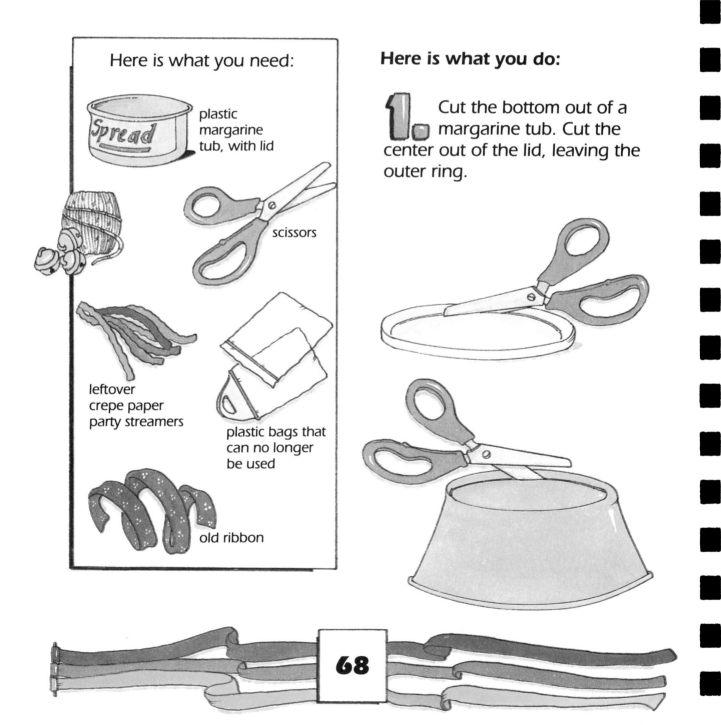

plastic margarine tub, with lid

scissors

leftover crepe paper party streamers

plastic bags that can no longer be used

old ribbon

Here is what you do:

1. Cut the bottom out of a margarine tub. Cut the center out of the lid, leaving the outer ring.

2. Cut 3-foot (1-meter) streamers from the crepe paper, ribbon, and plastic bags. Arrange them around the rim of the tub so that they hang down over the edge. Snap the lid over the rim of the tub to hold the streamers in place.

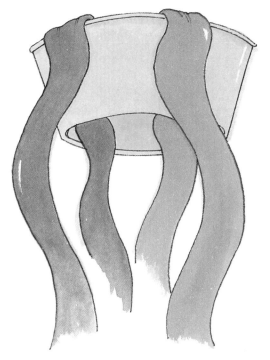

3. Tuck the two ends of a piece of ribbon under the lid so that it forms a hanger.

You can change or add to the streamers for your recycled wind sock as you find and save new things.

Oil Slick Paper

Oil will not mix with water. When it is spilled in our oceans it is a problem for both people and animals.

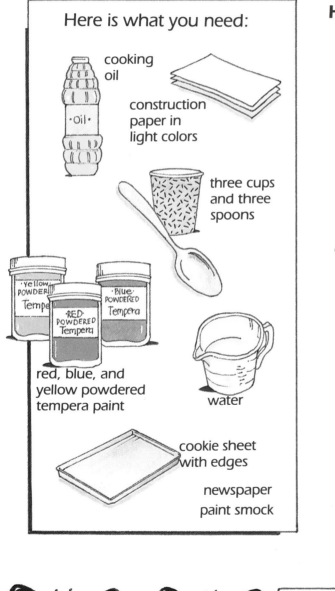

Here is what you need:

cooking oil

construction paper in light colors

three cups and three spoons

red, blue, and yellow powdered tempera paint

water

cookie sheet with edges

newspaper

paint smock

Here is what you do:

1. Spread out some newspaper to work on and to place your oily pictures on. Wear a paint smock to protect your clothing. Cover the bottom of a cookie sheet with water.

2. Pour about 1/4 cup of oil into each cup. Use about two tablespoons of powdered paint to color each cup of oil a different color. Mix each color well with a spoon.

3. Pour some of each color into the water in the pan. Swirl the colors together slightly with a spoon.

4. Carefully set a piece of paper down in the pan of water and colors. It will be ready to remove in just a few seconds. Pick it up at one end and let the excess water and oil run off. Then put it on a thick pad of newspaper to dry overnight. Each paper will be different as you stir the colors and add more oil and paint.

You can display your dried work as it is or cut it into pretty Earth Day shapes such as butterflies or flowers. Even when the paper is dry, it will be slightly oily, so it is best to display it taped to a window or another surface that can be wiped clean.

Earth Light Catcher

Here is what you need:

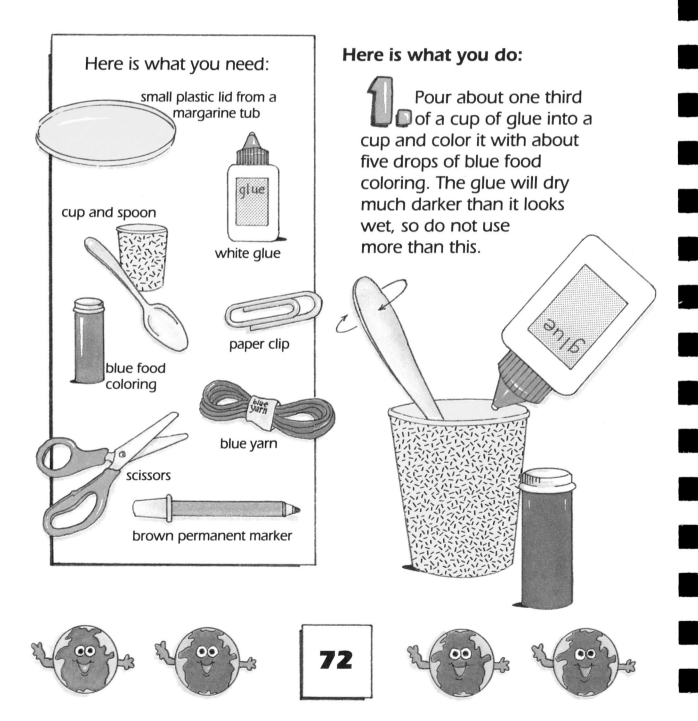

small plastic lid from a margarine tub

cup and spoon

white glue

blue food coloring

paper clip

blue yarn

scissors

brown permanent marker

Here is what you do:

1. Pour about one third of a cup of glue into a cup and color it with about five drops of blue food coloring. The glue will dry much darker than it looks wet, so do not use more than this.

2. Fill the plastic lid with the colored glue and set a paper clip in the glue to use as a hanger. Wash the cup and spoon immediately. Let the glue dry completely. This could take up to a week.

3. When the glue is totally dry, peel the blue circle out of the lid. Use a brown permanent marker to draw on landforms.

4. Tie a piece of blue yarn through the paper clip and hang the Earth in a sunny window.

Talking Earth Puppet

If our Earth could talk, what do you think it would tell us?

Here is what you need:

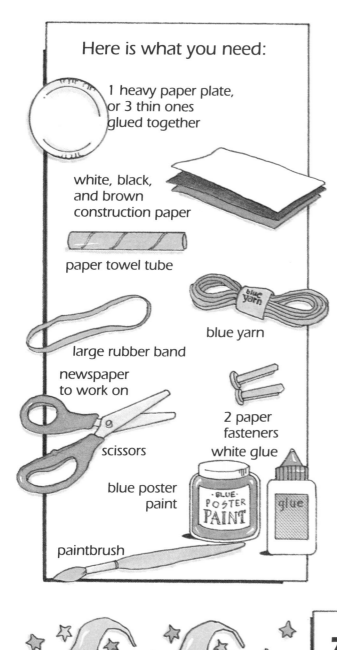

1 heavy paper plate, or 3 thin ones glued together

white, black, and brown construction paper

paper towel tube

blue yarn

large rubber band

newspaper to work on

2 paper fasteners

scissors

white glue

blue poster paint

paintbrush

Here is what you do:

1. Paint the bottom of the plate blue and let it dry.

2. Cut landforms from brown paper and glue them on the plate to make the Earth. Cut eyes from white and black paper and glue them in place. Poke the fasteners through the bottom of the plate far enough apart so that the rubber band will hook over each fastener to form the mouth of the puppet.

3. Tie a long piece of blue yarn to the bottom of the rubber band. Cut two slits in the top of a paper towel tube and slide the bottom of the Earth puppet into the slits so that you have a holder for the puppet. Drop the mouth string through the tube so that it hangs out the other end. To move the puppet's mouth just pull gently on the end of the yarn.

Let your puppet tell others how to love and care for our Earth.

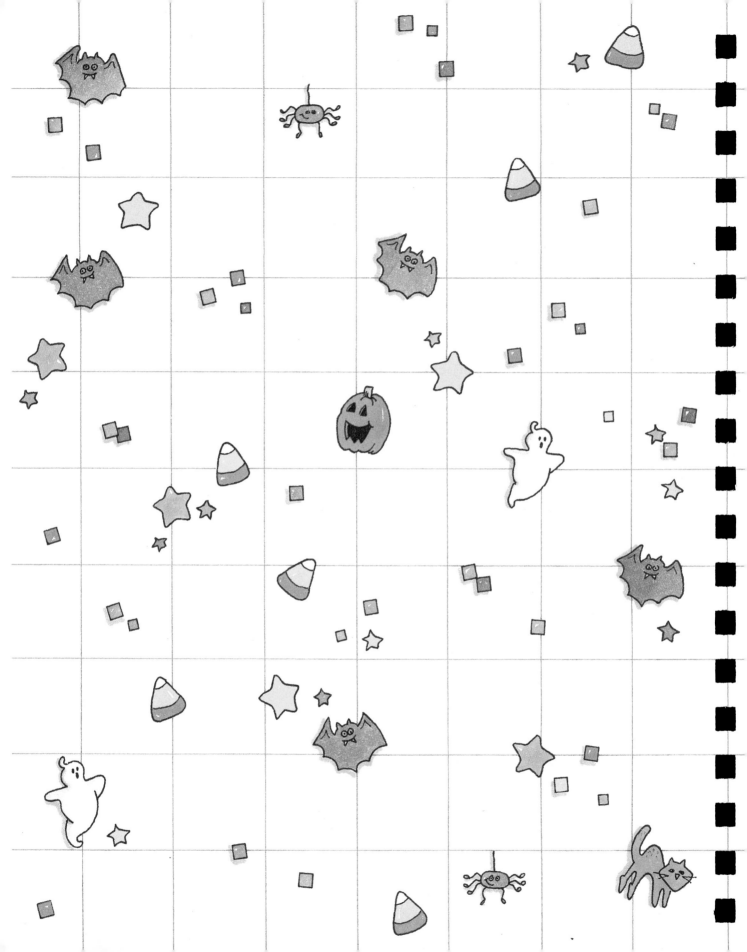

Happy Halloween!

On October 31, children in America celebrate Halloween. They dress up in costumes and go from house to house, asking for candy by saying "trick or treat." Some costumes are scary, some are silly, and others may be quite beautiful.

Long ago, people believed that spirits called ghosts wandered the earth, and they were afraid of these ghosts. Many of today's Halloween costumes have come from this old belief. Carved pumpkins and scary costumes were once used to try to frighten the spirits away. Today people place lighted pumpkins on their porches to welcome the children in their costumes.

Witches casting spells and flying around on broomsticks with their black cats, screeching owls, spiders, and swooping bats are all considered symbols of this spooky celebration. Halloween is a holiday for having a scary good time.

Sock Pumpkin

Pumpkins with carved faces and glowing candles inside are called jack-o'-lanterns. Here are some pumpkins that you can make.

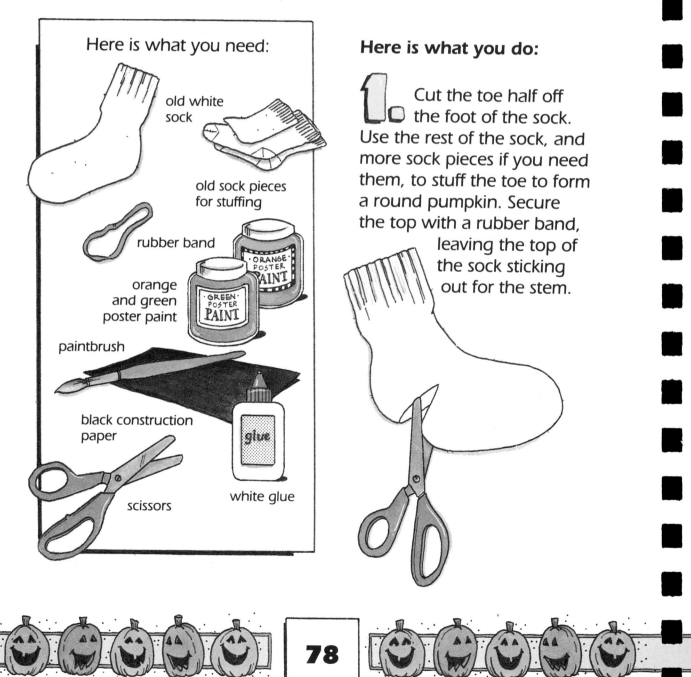

Here is what you need:

old white sock

old sock pieces for stuffing

rubber band

orange and green poster paint

paintbrush

black construction paper

scissors

white glue

Here is what you do:

1. Cut the toe half off the foot of the sock. Use the rest of the sock, and more sock pieces if you need them, to stuff the toe to form a round pumpkin. Secure the top with a rubber band, leaving the top of the sock sticking out for the stem.

2. Paint the pumpkin orange and the stem green. Twist the stem while it is wet so it will dry in the shape of a stem. When the paint is dry, glue on a jack-o'-lantern face cut from black paper.

GREEN POSTER PAINT

ORANGE POSTER PAINT

glue

The size of each pumpkin you make will be determined by the size of the sock it is made from. Several stuffed pumpkins can be displayed together with green yarn and paper leaves entwined among them to look like a pumpkin patch.

Talking Pumpkin Puppet

Ask an adult to help you make this pumpkin puppet.

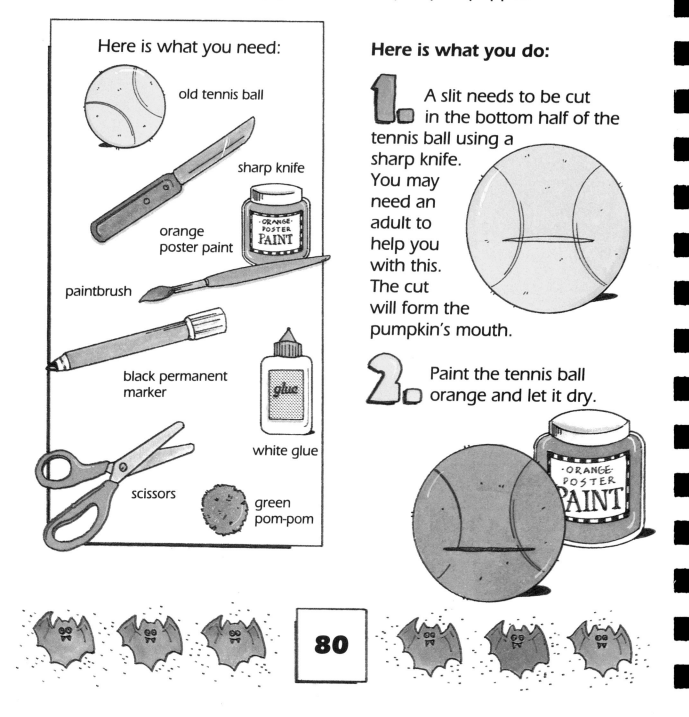

Here is what you need:

old tennis ball

sharp knife

orange poster paint

ORANGE POSTER PAINT

paintbrush

black permanent marker

glue

white glue

scissors

green pom-pom

Here is what you do:

1. A slit needs to be cut in the bottom half of the tennis ball using a sharp knife. You may need an adult to help you with this. The cut will form the pumpkin's mouth.

2. Paint the tennis ball orange and let it dry.

ORANGE POSTER PAINT

3. Use a black marker to draw a mouth around the slit cut in the ball, and add a pumpkin nose and eyes. Glue a green pom-pom on top of the ball for a stem. To make your pumpkin talk just place a finger on each side of the mouth and squeeze. The mouth will open and close when you do this.

Talking pumpkins make great party favors because they can be filled through the cut mouth with candy and small surprises.

Milk Carton Witch

Witches like to turn people into toads, but you can turn a milk carton and an egg carton into a witch.

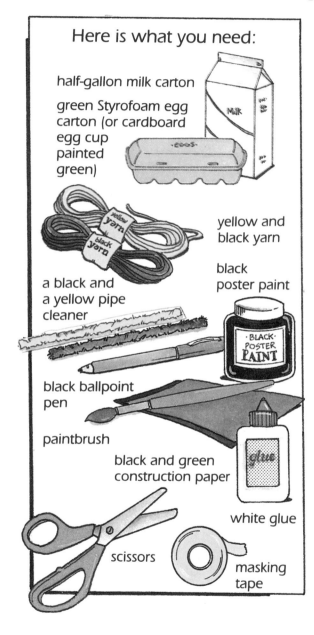

Here is what you need:

half-gallon milk carton

green Styrofoam egg carton (or cardboard egg cup painted green)

yellow and black yarn

black poster paint

a black and a yellow pipe cleaner

black ballpoint pen

paintbrush

black and green construction paper

white glue

scissors

masking tape

Here is what you do:

1. Cut the top off the milk carton just below the place where it starts to fold in to form the spout. You will need the top part of the carton to make the witch. (Hint: Save the bottom to make the Haunted House Treat Carrier on page 22.) Paint the milk carton top with black paint. If you use poster paint, you will need to cover the surface with masking tape, or the paint will not stick.

2. Cut one cup from the egg carton. Push it partway through the open spout of the milk carton and glue it in place to form the witch's face. Poke a piece of yellow pipe cleaner through the middle of the face to make a nose. Then draw on eyes and a mouth using a ballpoint pen. Glue long pieces of unraveled black yarn around the face for hair.

3. Make a broom for the witch to hold by tying several pieces of yellow yarn to one end of a black pipe cleaner. Cut two hands from green construction paper. Glue them on the front of the witch, with the broom between them.

4. Trace around the back (open) portion of the witch on black paper. Cut out the square shape and glue it over the opening.

If you are giving your witch to someone as a gift, you can write a Halloween greeting on orange paper and glue it on the back of the witch. If you are using her as a party favor, she can be filled with goodies before you cover the back.

BOO!

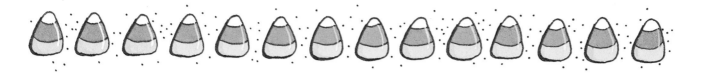

Yowling Cat Puppet

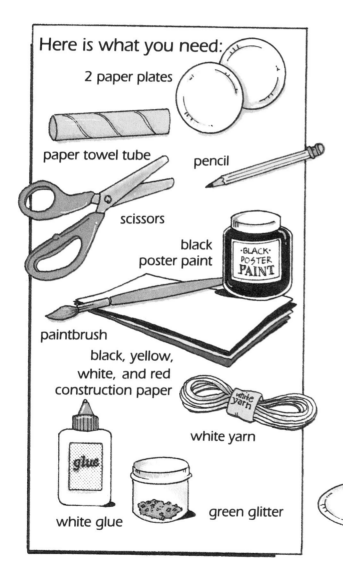

Here is what you need:

2 paper plates

paper towel tube

pencil

scissors

black poster paint

·BLACK· POSTER PAINT

paintbrush

black, yellow, white, and red construction paper

white yarn

glue

white glue

green glitter

Here is what you do:

1. Trace a round mouth on the bottom half of a paper plate, using the end of the paper towel tube as a pattern. Hold both plates together and cut out the circle from both. Spread glue on the top of one plate and the bottom of the other one. Cut slits all the way around one end of the tube and spread the pieces out to the sides. Put this over the hole of the plate with glue on the bottom.

Then slide on the other plate and press the two plates together so that the slit flaps are sandwiched between them. The tube will act as a megaphone to make your cat puppet yowl in a spooky way.

2. Wait until your puppet is completely dry before continuing. You may need to weight the plates with books to make sure they dry completely stuck together.

3. Paint the front of the puppet black. Cut triangle ears from black paper and glue them on. Cut cat eyes from yellow and black paper. To give them a very spooky look, use green glitter to make the centers. Glue a black pupil in the center of each eye. Line the mouth with a piece of red construction paper. Cut sharp teeth from the white paper and glue them around the mouth opening. Glue on some yarn whiskers.

After following steps one and two you might choose to make a different Halloween character, such as a bat, a witch, or a goblin Use your own ideas to create lots of different puppets.

Haunted House Treat Carrier

Make a haunted house for your Halloween goodies.

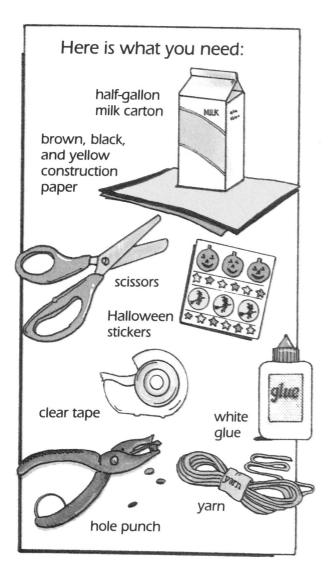

Here is what you need:

half-gallon milk carton

brown, black, and yellow construction paper

scissors

Halloween stickers

clear tape

white glue

hole punch

yarn

Here is what you do:

1. Cut the top off the milk carton just below the place where it starts to fold in to form the spout. You will need the bottom part for this project. Cover the carton with yellow paper cut to fit, and tape it in place.

2. Cut a piece of brown paper to cover the yellow paper. Hold it in place over the yellow paper and draw a front door and several windows. Remove the brown paper and cut the door and windows on three sides so that they open and shut. Tape the brown paper back in place over the yellow paper.

3. Cut nine long strands of yarn in one or more colors to make the handle. Punch two holes on opposite sides of the carton and tie the strings through one of the holes. Braid the strands together to make a strong handle for your treat carrier. Then knot the ends through the hole on the other side of the carton.

4. Open all your doors and windows and put a Halloween sticker inside each. Use a black marker to add details to the outside of your house. You may even want to put a ghost sticker or two on the outside to give it that haunted look. Cut a roof from black paper to glue on the front of the house.

You can draw your own spooky ideas for Halloween characters in your house instead of using Halloween stickers.

Floating Ghosts

Haunt your house with these Halloween ghosts.

Here is what you need:

a lid from a small jar

half a Styrofoam ball, small enough to fit inside lid

5 Styrofoam packing worms

5 squares of bathroom tissue

5 white or black pipe cleaners

black marker

white glue

masking tape

paintbrush

black poster paint

Here is what you do:

1. Cover the rim of the lid with masking tape so that you can paint it. Glue the half of the Styrofoam ball in the lid. Paint the ball and the edge of the lid black.

·BLACK· POSTER PAINT

This is the base for your ghosts.

2. To make each ghost, rub glue on the sides and end of a Styrofoam packing worm and loosely cover it with a square of bathroom tissue. Make five ghosts. Give each ghost a spooky face with a black marker.

3. Stick one end of a pipe cleaner into glue and then into the bottom of one of your ghosts. Stick the other end into the Styrofoam base. Do this with all your ghosts, and arrange them to look as if they are floating about.

Hairpin Ghost Necklace

Here is what you need:

plastic lid from margarine container or coffee can

hairpin

scraps of black construction paper

black thread

white glue

scissors

Here is what you do:

1. Spread the hairpin apart slightly so that it forms the outline of a ghost. Tie a long black thread around the top of the hairpin. Then tie the two ends of the thread together to make a necklace.

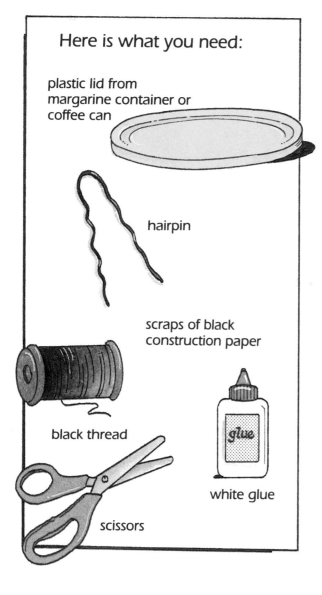

2. Set the hairpin on a plastic margarine lid and use a squeeze bottle of white glue to fill the area inside the hairpin. Cut tiny round eyes and a mouth from black paper and stick them in the glue near the top of the hairpin for the ghost's face.

3. Place the lid on a completely flat surface to keep the glue from running out of the hairpin, and allow the ghost to dry completely. When the glue is dry, peel the ghost off the lid. Trim off any extra glue that has run over the sides or too far from the bottom of the ghost.

When you aren't wearing your little ghost around your neck, you can hang it in a window. It will look very spooky with the light shining through it.

91

Little Ghost
Table Decoration

Here is what you need:

clear disposable plastic cup

two Styrofoam packing worms

green pipe cleaner

black construction paper

one square of bathroom tissue

black marker

orange permanent marker

scissors

white glue

Here is what you do:

1. Trace around the rim of the cup on black paper, and cut the circle out.

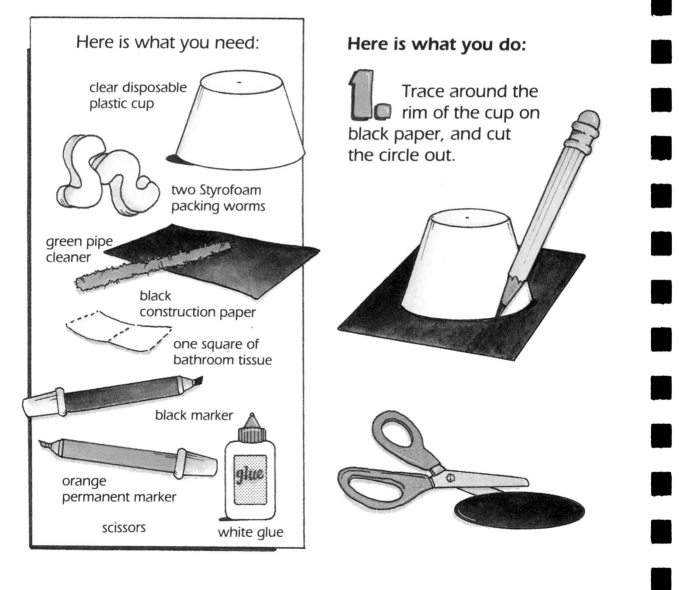

2. Make the ghost by dipping one end of a Styrofoam packing worm in glue and then covering it with a square of bathroom tissue. Give the ghost a face with a black marker.

3. Make the pumpkin by cutting the end off another packing worm and coloring it orange. Poke a piece of green pipe cleaner in the top for the stem.

4. Glue the ghost and the pumpkin to the black circle. Let the glue dry completely before continuing. (If you don't, you will have moisture inside the cup.) Dip the rim of the cup in glue and set it over the circle so that the ghost and pumpkin are inside the cup.

If you store this decoration carefully you will have it to enjoy for many Halloweens to come.

Stuffed Sock Bat

Make a bat to hang around your house this Halloween.

Here is what you need:

old black sock

stuffing (crumpled newspaper or cotton balls)

NEWSPAPER

scissors

white glue

black and white felt or construction paper

pipe cleaners

red and black yarn

Here is what you do:

1. Stuff the foot of a black sock and tie the end with black yarn. Tie the two ends of the yarn together so that you will be able to hang your bat upside down. Trim off the excess sock.

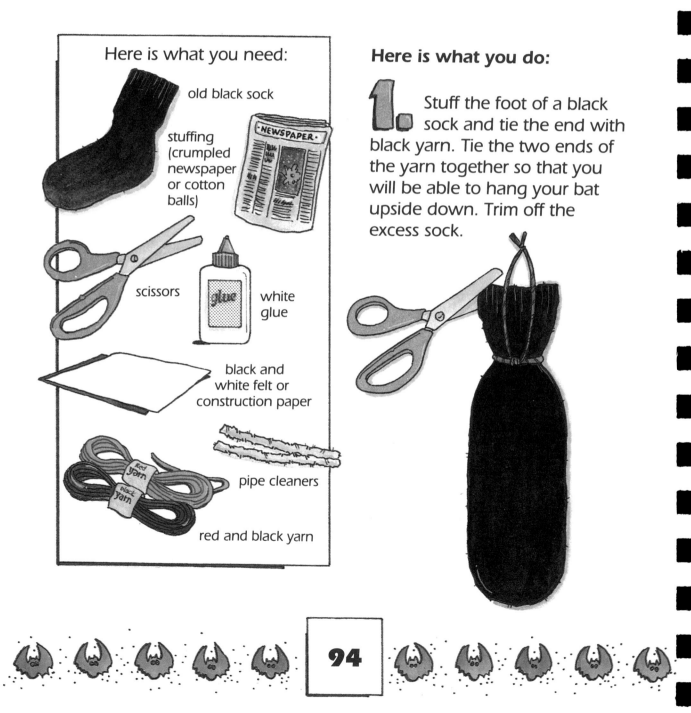

2. Cut eyes, ears, and teeth from the felt or paper and glue them at the toe end of the sock. Give your bat a smile cut from the red yarn. For each wing, cut a front and a back piece from the black felt or paper. Glue each front and back together with two or three pipe cleaners in between, so that the wings can be bent in different shapes. Glue the two wings to the back of your bat so that they stick out, and hang the bat upside down (bats' favorite position) to dry.

Spider Web

Eek! Spiders!

Here is what you need:

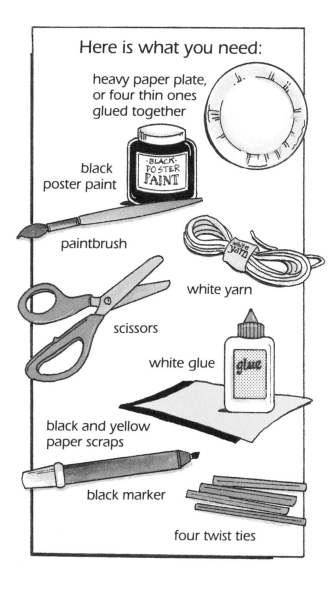

heavy paper plate, or four thin ones glued together

black poster paint

paintbrush

white yarn

scissors

white glue

black and yellow paper scraps

black marker

four twist ties

Here is what you do:

1. Cut several small slits, evenly spaced, around the edge of the paper plate. Paint the plate black. When it is dry, wrap white yarn around and around the plate to form a spider web, securing it in the slits around the edge. Leave one end of the yarn hanging off the web, so you will have a place to attach your spider. Tie the other end in a loop, so you can hang up your web.

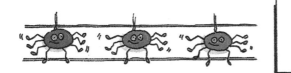

2. To make a spider, cut two circles of the same size from black paper. Cover one circle with glue and place four twist ties across the circle so that they stick out on each side to form the spider's legs. Add more glue, and cover the first circle with the second circle. Bend the twist ties to form knees and feet for the spider. Glue on eyes cut from yellow paper and draw a dot in the middle of each one with a black marker.

3. Attach your spider to the end of the yarn web by putting the loose end of the yarn between the two circles. Let the glue dry completely. Then hang your spider web on your front door. Your spider can hang out on his web or swing from it.

Newspaper Owl

Here is what you need:

8 double sheets of newspaper, plus extra newspaper for stuffing

stapler

2 large and 2 small paper plates

paintbrush

brown, orange, and black poster paint

black and orange construction paper

scissors

white glue

Here is what you do:

1. Open eight double sheets of newspaper and stack them on top of each other. Staple them all together around the top, bottom, and one side, leaving the last side open like a bag. Open the newspaper bag up so that four sheets are on one side and four on the other. Stuff the bag with crumpled newspaper. Staple the open side shut.

2. Paint the newspaper owl brown on both sides. If you do not have a large paintbrush, you can use a sponge to spread the paint quickly.

3. To make the eyes, paint two small paper plates orange and glue one on top of each of the large paper plates. Cut two pupils for the eyes from black paper and glue one in the center of each of the orange plates. Glue the eyes on the top part of the owl. Cut a triangle beak from orange construction paper, and glue it on under the eyes. Use black paint to draw the outline of wings on each side of the owl's body.

This owl is so big it will need a chair of its own!

Monster Man

Mad scientists make monsters in their laboratories.
You can make one, too!

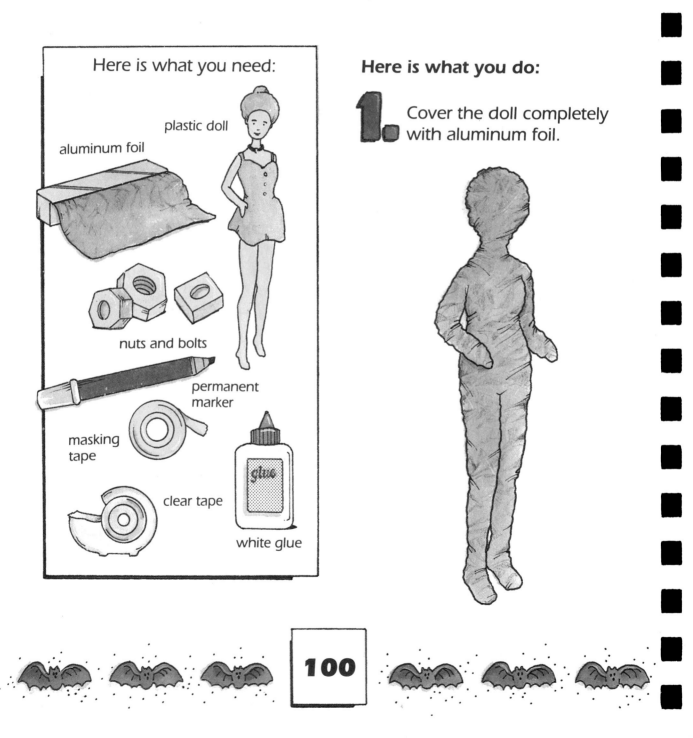

Here is what you need:

plastic doll

aluminum foil

nuts and bolts

permanent marker

masking tape

clear tape

white glue

Here is what you do:

1. Cover the doll completely with aluminum foil.

2. Glue on nuts and bolts for facial features and controls. Put a tiny piece of masking tape under each place where you want to glue so that the metal will stick better. Heavier bolts may need clear tape to hold them on. Use a permanent marker to add details.

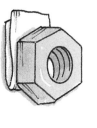

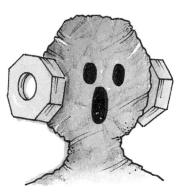

You can also turn your doll into a mummy, by wrapping it completely with toilet tissue. Don't forget to leave the eyes peeking out. After Halloween, just remove the foil or tissue, and you'll have your doll friend back again.

Happy Thanksgiving!

Thanksgiving is celebrated in the United States on the third Thursday of November and in Canada on the second Monday in October. It is a time when friends and family like to celebrate and give thanks for the blessings of the year.

In New England the first traditional Thanksgiving was celebrated by the Plymouth colonists. These early settlers, called Pilgrims, had come to America in the 1600s to escape religious persecution. Their first winter in their new home had been very hard. Native Americans showed the Pilgrims how to grow the corn they needed to survive the difficult winters. Together the Pilgrims and the Native Americans celebrated and gave thanks for a good harvest. This harvest festival began the Thanksgiving Day tradition.

Today Thanksgiving is celebrated by families and friends enjoying a big Thanksgiving meal. The Thanksgiving meal usually includes roast turkey with lots of delicious side dishes. Many families set aside some time to give thanks just as the Pilgrims and Native Americans did so many years ago.

I am thankful for my mom and dad!

Headband Napkin Rings

Native Americans shared the first Thanksgiving with the Pilgrims.
Make these napkin rings to use at your Thanksgiving celebration.

Here is what you need:

cardboard paper towel tube

construction paper scraps

markers

scissors

white glue

Here is what you do:

1. Cut a cardboard circle from the tube, about 3/4 inch (20 centimeters) wide for each napkin ring you want to make.

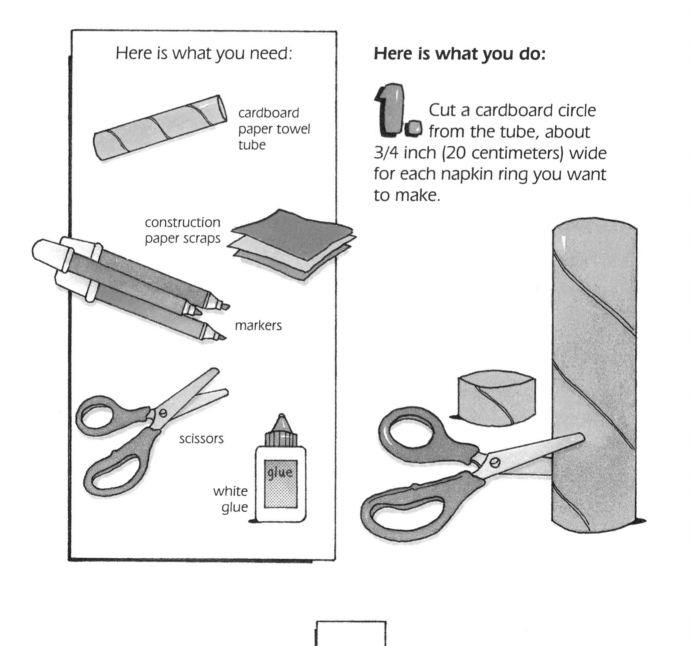

2. Use markers to draw a Native American design on the tube.

3. Cut a tiny feather from construction paper. Fringe both sides to make it look more featherlike. Glue the base of the feather inside the band.

Make lots of napkin rings using different designs and colors.

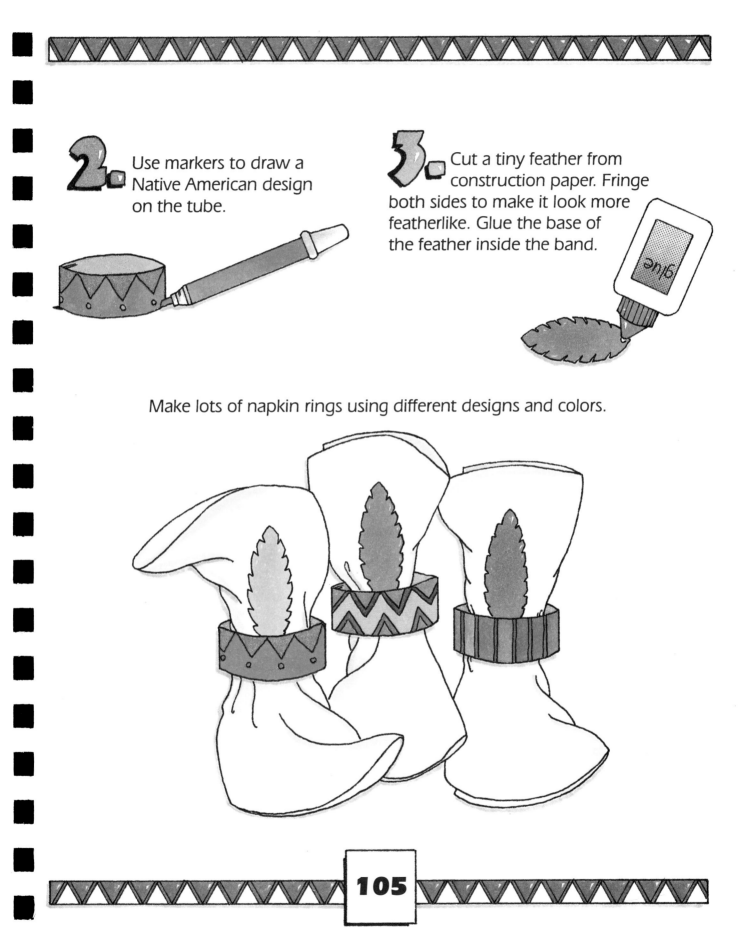

Boy Pilgrim Hat Favor

Make Pilgrim hat favors for everyone at your Thanksgiving table.

Here is what you need:

paper cup

black, blue, and orange construction paper

black yarn

scissors

white glue

small treats

Here is what you do:

1. Cut the bottom out of a paper cup. Cover the outside of the cup with glue and wrap the cup in black yarn until it is completely covered.

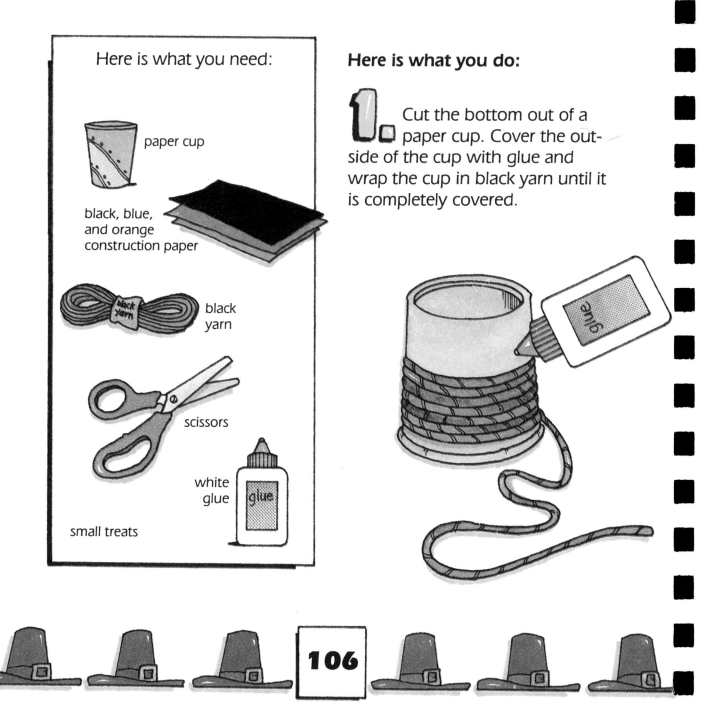

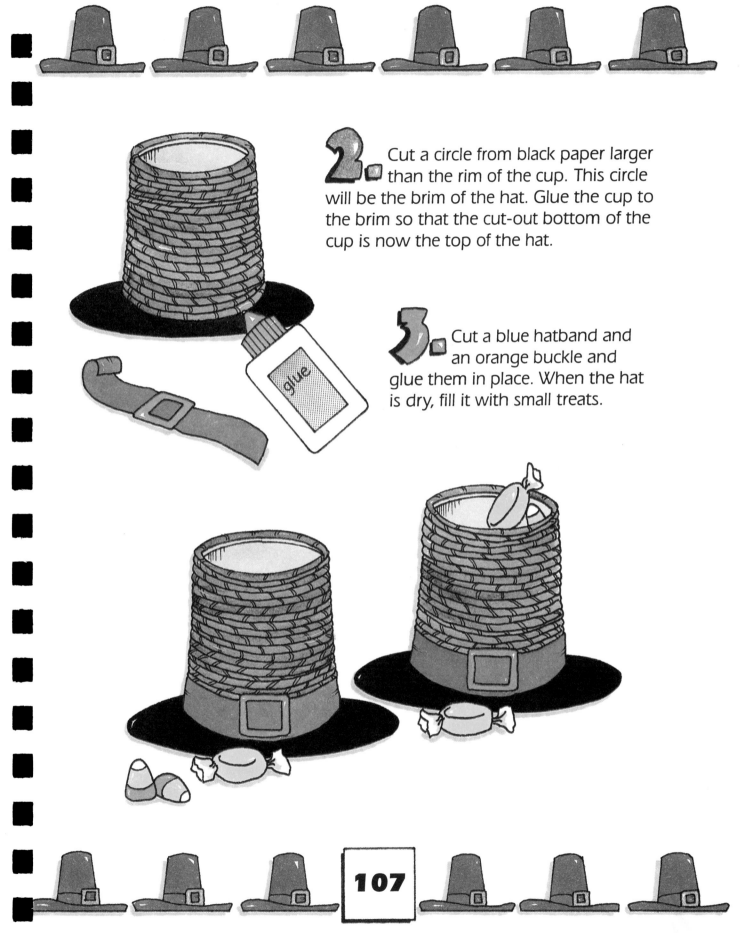

2. Cut a circle from black paper larger than the rim of the cup. This circle will be the brim of the hat. Glue the cup to the brim so that the cut-out bottom of the cup is now the top of the hat.

3. Cut a blue hatband and an orange buckle and glue them in place. When the hat is dry, fill it with small treats.

Girl Pilgrim Hat Favor

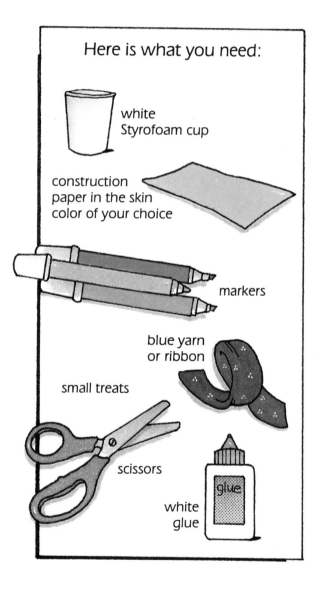

Here is what you need:

white Styrofoam cup

construction paper in the skin color of your choice

markers

blue yarn or ribbon

small treats

scissors

white glue

Here is what you do:

1. Cut a circle from construction paper slightly larger than the opening of the cup. Draw a face in the middle of the circle and then draw hair around the face.

2. Fill the cup with treats wrapped in plastic wrap. Rub glue around the inside edge of the cup. Place the face over the opening of the cup and tuck the edges down around the treats.

3. Glue a yarn bow at the chin of the face. When the glue has dried, set the favor on its side.

glue

Soft Sculpture Turkey

The traditional bird of Thanksgiving is the turkey. Make this little turkey to decorate a corner of your home.

Here is what you need:

craft feathers

old knit glove

two eyes that wiggle

scraps of red and orange felt

cotton balls

scissors

white glue

Here is what you do:

1. Stuff the glove with cotton balls. Turn the edges inside and glue them together. You may need to hold the edges shut until they are dry. You can do this with a large paper clip or a clamping clothespin.

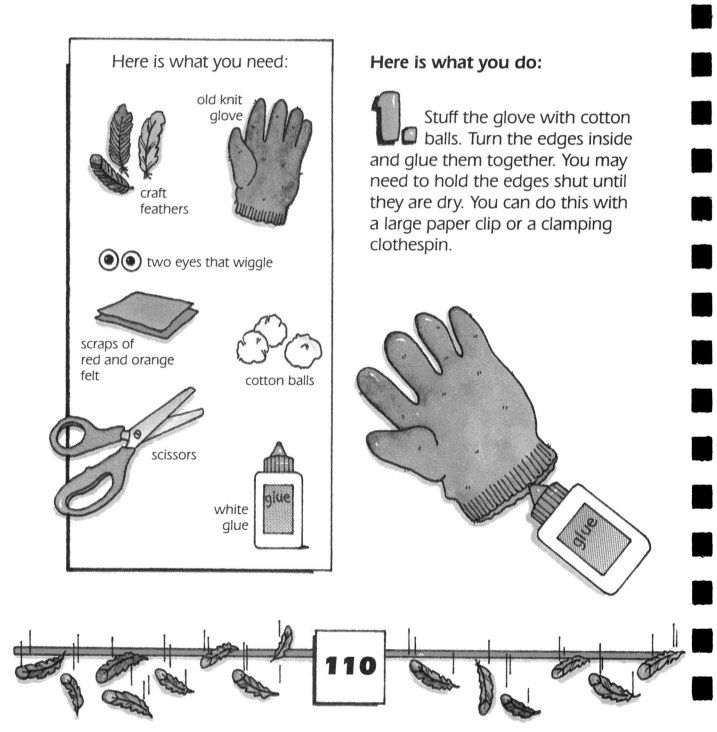

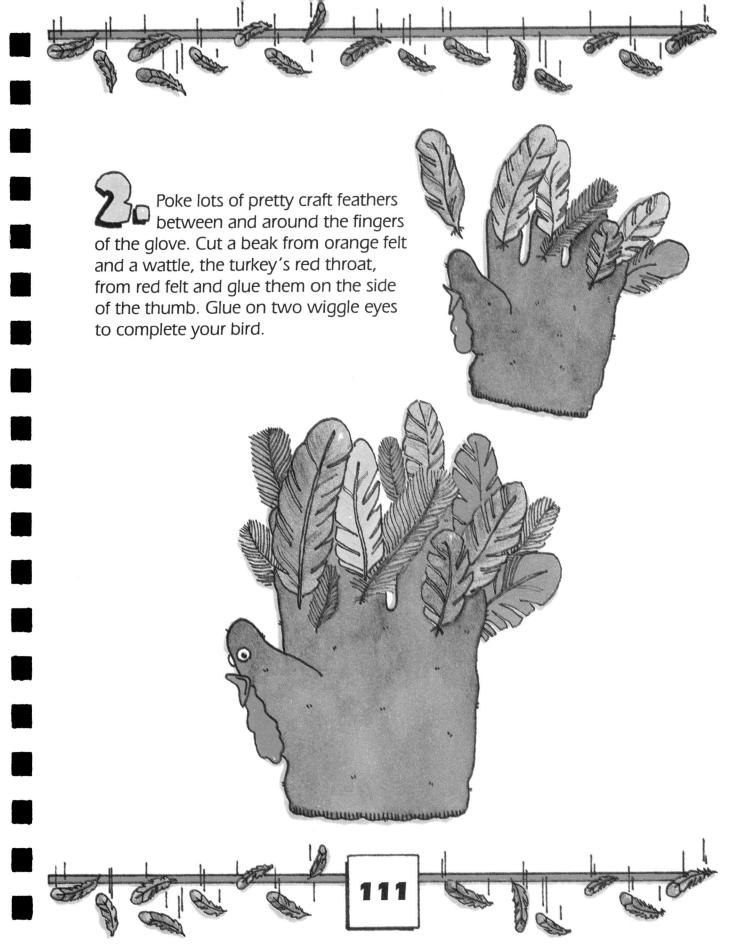

2. Poke lots of pretty craft feathers between and around the fingers of the glove. Cut a beak from orange felt and a wattle, the turkey's red throat, from red felt and glue them on the side of the thumb. Glue on two wiggle eyes to complete your bird.

Turkey Wreath

This turkey is to hang on your front door.

Here is what you need:

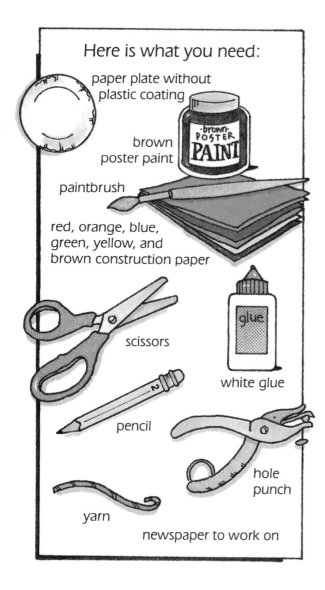

paper plate without plastic coating

brown poster paint

paintbrush

red, orange, blue, green, yellow, and brown construction paper

scissors

white glue

pencil

hole punch

yarn

newspaper to work on

Here is what you do:

1. Cut the center out of a paper plate so that the rim forms a wreath. Paint the rim brown and let it dry. Punch a hole in the plate and tie a loop of yarn through for a hanger.

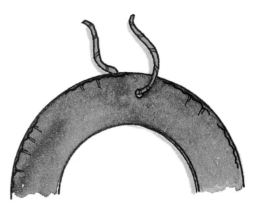

2. Cut a head for the turkey from brown paper and glue it to the bottom front

of the wreath. Cut eyes, a beak, and a wattle from paper and glue them in place on the head. Cut legs from orange paper and glue them so that they hang below the head.

3. To make feathers for the turkey, cut lots of 4-inch (10-centimeter) strips from different colors of paper. Wrap each strip tightly around a pencil and carefully slide the pencil out of the rolled paper. Fill the entire wreath with paper curls.

Gobble, gobble!

Hands and Feet Turkey

Surprise someone this Thanksgiving with a turkey
made from your own hands and feet.

Here is what you need:

green, yellow, and orange construction paper

red, blue, and brown construction paper

white glue

pencil

scissors

Here is what you do:

1. On brown paper, trace both your feet. Cut the paper feet out. Glue the feet together at the heel, so that the feet fan out at the toes. This will be the body of the turkey.

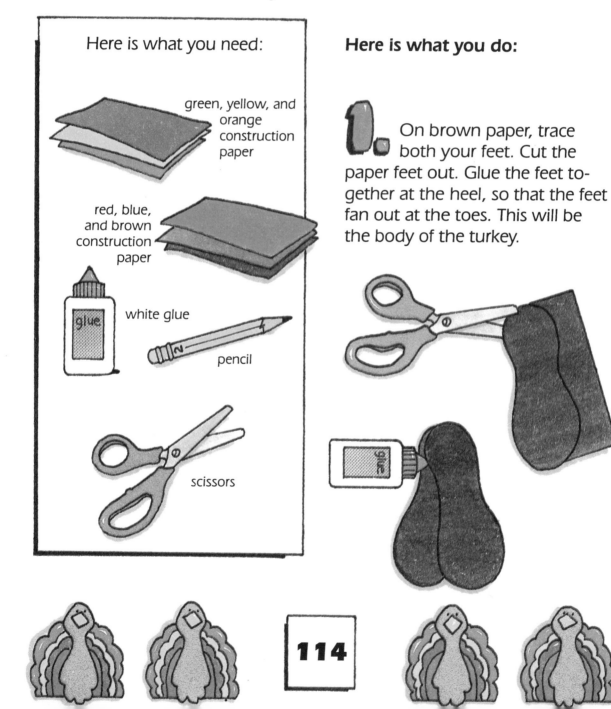

2. Cut out eyes, a beak, and a wattle, and glue them to the head of the turkey (the heels). Cut out two orange turkey legs and glue them to the bottom of the turkey.

3. Trace your hand on green, yellow, red, blue, and orange paper. Cut out three orange hands and one hand from each of the other colors. Glue one orange hand on each side of the turkey for wings. Fan out the other five hands and glue them behind the turkey to form the tail.

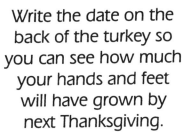

Write the date on the back of the turkey so you can see how much your hands and feet will have grown by next Thanksgiving.

House Napkin Holder

Here is what you need:

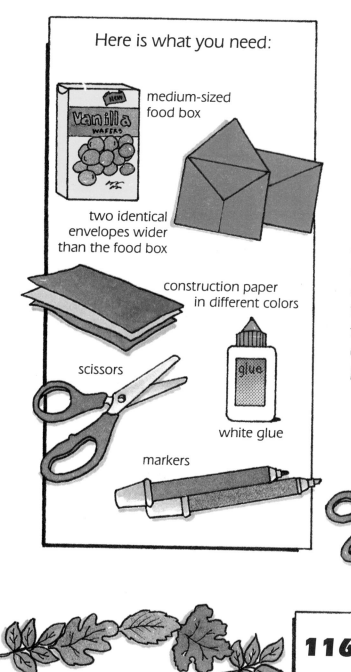

medium-sized food box

two identical envelopes wider than the food box

construction paper in different colors

scissors

white glue

markers

Here is what you do:

1. Open the flap of one envelope so that it looks like a house. If the envelopes are white, you might want to color them with markers. Place one envelope so that it overlaps the food box slightly on each side. Trace around the pointed flap of the envelope and follow the lines to cut away the portion of the box above the envelope flap. Do the same thing on the other side of the box. Cut away both sides of the box leaving only about 1/4 inch (6 millimeters) at the bottom.

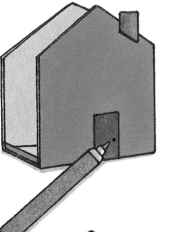

 2. Glue an envelope to each side of the box. Cut paper to fit inside the napkin holder to line it and glue the paper in place.

 3. Cut doors, windows, and chimneys from construction paper and draw details with markers. Glue these to both sides of the house.

 4. Let this project dry with one side of the house facedown.

Fill the house with napkins and surprise someone with this useful gift.

Play Food

You can pretend to serve your own Thanksgiving dinner as well as other favorite meals if you make a set of play food.

Here is what you need:

pictures of foods from magazines and supermarket flyers

white glue

scissors

construction paper

clear Con-Tact paper

Here is what you do:

1. Cut out pictures of lots of different kinds of foods. Choose pictures that are about the same size. Carefully cut out only the food, with no background, from each picture.

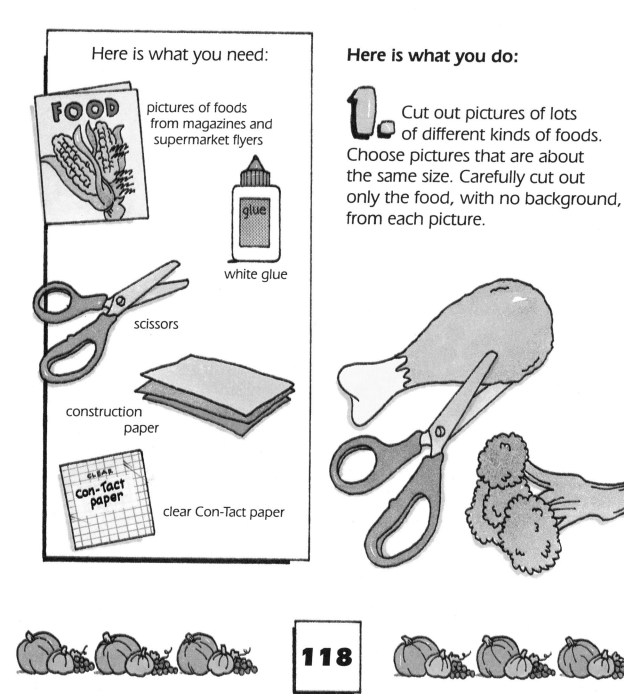

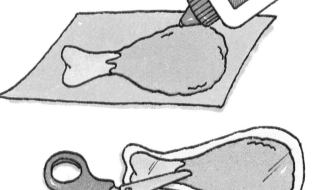

 Glue each picture to construction paper. Let it dry and cut it out.

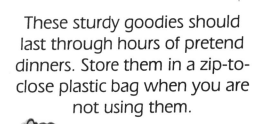

Cover both sides of each picture with a slightly larger piece of clear Con-Tact paper. Carefully cut out each food item again.

These sturdy goodies should last through hours of pretend dinners. Store them in a zip-to-close plastic bag when you are not using them.

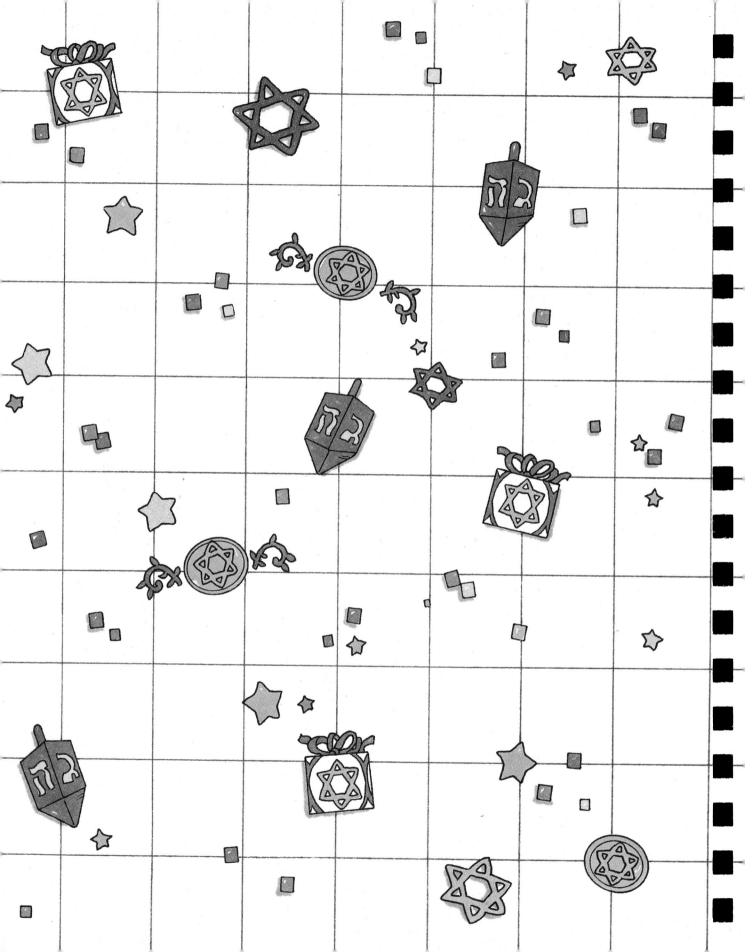

Happy Hanukkah!

Hanukkah is an eight-day Jewish holiday celebration that begins on the twenty-fifth day of the month of Kislev in the Jewish calendar. The first day of Hanukkah usually falls in December.

The word Hanukkah means dedication. This holiday remembers the restoration, over two thousand years ago, of a temple in Jerusalem lost to a powerful enemy of the Jews for three years and then reclaimed. According to legend, the Jewish soldiers, led by Judah Maccabee, found only enough oil in the temple to burn a lamp for one day, but the lamp burned for eight days.

Some of the traditions of Hanukkah include lighting a candle on a *menorah* for each of the eight days of Hanukkah, giving gifts or *gelt* (real or chocolate money), and playing games with spinning tops called *dreidels*. *Latkes*, potato pancakes fried in oil and served with applesauce, is a traditional Hanukkah dish.

Aluminum Foil Menorah

Light your Hanukkah season with this sparkling menorah.

Here is what you need:

shoe box lid

aluminum foil

18 foil cupcake wrappers

cereal-box cardboard

masking tape

blue glitter

metallic rickrack or other trim

white glue

scissors

nine candles, 10 inches (25.4 centimeters) high

Here is what you do:

1. Cut nine circles out of the cardboard. They should be about 1½ inches (3.75 centimeters) wide. Place one circle in the bottom center of a foil cupcake wrapper. Put another foil wrapper inside, on top of the cardboard circle.

2. Put one of the candles in the center of the wrappers and press the sides of the wrappers flat around the cardboard circle and up around the candle. This makes the holder for one candle. You need to make eight more holders.

 To make the base of the menorah, cover the top and sides of the shoe box lid with aluminum foil. Put a strip of masking tape along the sides of the lid. Cover the masking tape with glue, and then sprinkle the glue with blue glitter. Let the glue dry.

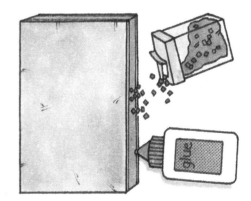

 Run a line of glue around the middle of the glittered rim and glue on metallic trim. Let the glue dry.

A *shamash* is the candle used to light the other candles. Stand the shamash by itself to the far right of the base. Stand the other eight candles in two rows, staggering them slightly. Put a square of masking tape on the base where each candle will stand. Put a square of masking tape on the bottom of each candle holder and some glue on the tape. Glue each candle holder in place on the base and put the candles in the holders.

Place your menorah in a window to remind all who see it of a great miracle.

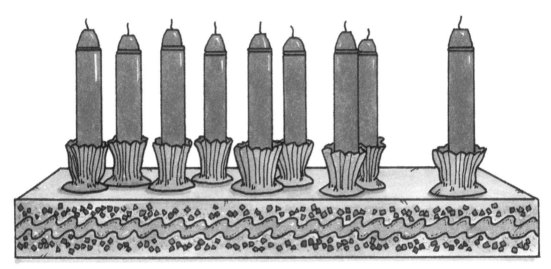

Hanukkah Match Holder

Keep the matches for lighting the menorah
safe and handy with this match holder.

Here is what you need:

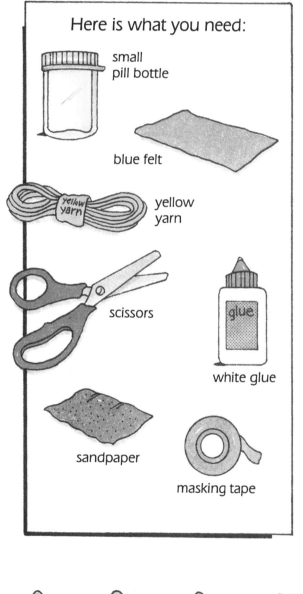

small
pill bottle

blue felt

yellow
yarn

scissors

white glue

sandpaper

masking tape

Here is what you do:

1. Cut a piece of blue felt long
and wide enough to cover
the outside of the pill bottle. The
ends should overlap slightly so that
you can glue them together.

2. Cut six 1-inch (2.5-centimeter) pieces of yarn and glue them to the side of the holder in the shape of a Star of David. Glue a longer band of yellow yarn along the edges of the felt, at the top and the bottom of the holder.

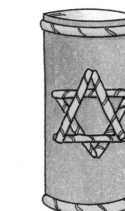

3. Cut a circle of sandpaper the size of the bottom of the bottle. The sandpaper is used to strike the matches. Glue won't stick to plastic, so you need to put a square of masking tape on the bottom of the bottle before you glue the sandpaper circle in place.

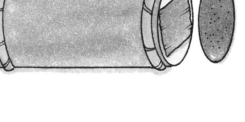

Give this match holder to the grown-up in your house who is in charge of lighting the candles.

Envelope Dreidel Card

A dreidel is a four-sided toy, marked with Hebrew letters, that is spun like a top. But this dreidel is not for spinning. It's for delivering a special Hanukkah greeting.

Here is what you need:

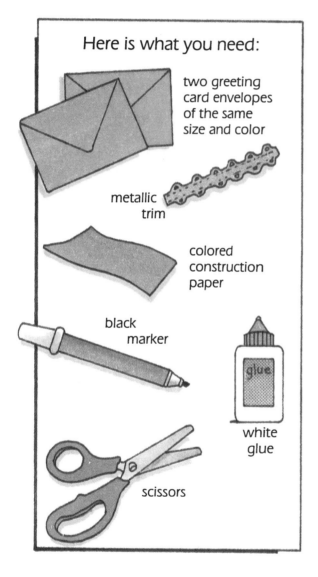

two greeting card envelopes of the same size and color

metallic trim

colored construction paper

black marker

white glue

scissors

Here is what you do:

1. Open the flaps of the envelopes. Put glue along the sides of the back of the envelopes and along the outer edges of the flaps.

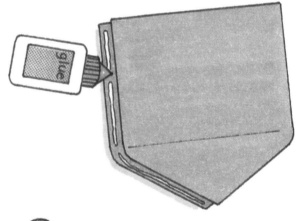

2. With the backs of the envelopes facing each other, glue the flaps and sides together. This will make a dreidel shape with a pocket inside.

3. Cut a handle for the dreidel from construction paper. It should be long enough to slide all the way into the pocket to the point of the envelope, leaving a 4-inch (10-centimeter) handle sticking out of the other end.

Write your Hanukkah message on the part of the handle that will be hidden. Write PULL at the top end of the handle and slide the message part of the handle into the dreidel pocket.

4. If you used white envelopes instead of colored ones, you may want to color the dreidel with markers or crayons. Draw a Hebrew letter—*Nun, Gimel, Hay,* or *Shin*—on the front of the dreidel with a black marker. Decorate the dreidel and handle by gluing on strips of metallic trim.

Wish someone you know a very happy Hanukkah with this unusual greeting card!

Dreidel Pin

This dreidel won't spin around, but it looks wonderful pinned on a shirt or coat.

Here is what you need:

old necktie

cotton swab

white glue

aluminum foil

small safety pin

scissors

thin trim or ribbon in blue or silver

Here is what you do:

1. Cut a piece off the narrow end of an old necktie, about 2 inches (5 centimeters) above the point, to make the dreidel.

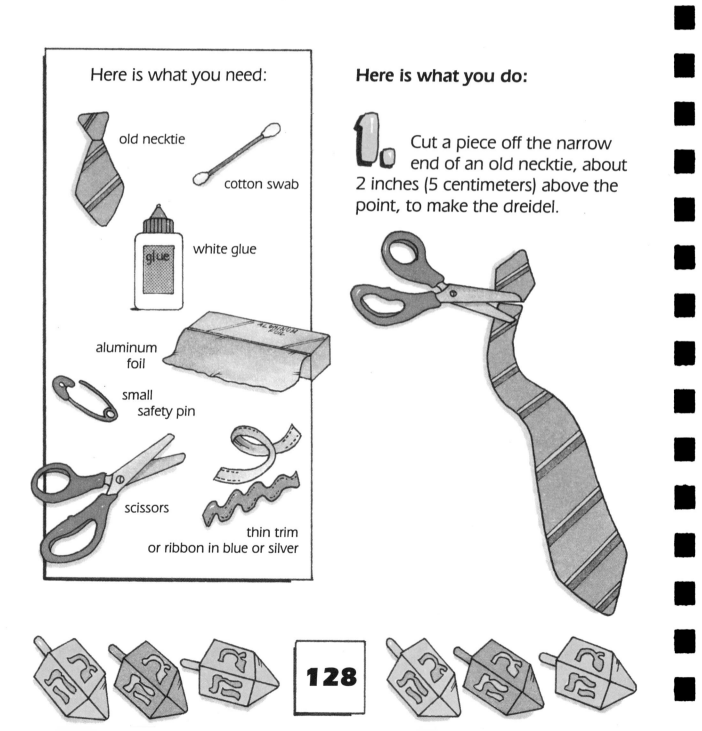

2. Cut the cotton swab in half. Cover the cotton end of one of the halves with aluminum foil to make a handle for the dreidel. Cover the stick end of the handle with glue. Slip the stick between the front and back layers of fabric at the top of the dreidel.(Glue the fabric at the back of the dreidel together if it came unsewn when it was cut from the end of the tie.)

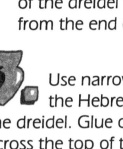

3. Use narrow trim to make one of the Hebrew letters on the front of the dreidel. Glue one or more rows of trim across the top of the dreidel.

4. Attach a small safety pin to the back of the dreidel so that it can be pinned onto a shirt, jacket, or dress.

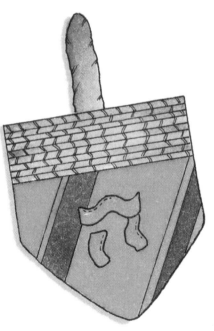

This dreidel also makes a very nice magnet for your refrigerator door. Instead of putting a safety pin on the back, press on a piece of sticky-back magnetic strip.

Kiddush Cup Necklace

This kiddush cup is to wear.

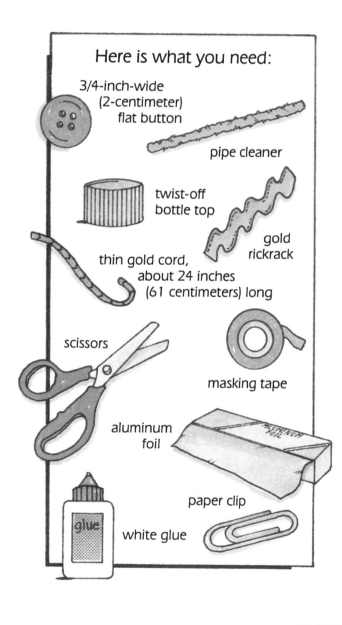

Here is what you need:

3/4-inch-wide (2-centimeter) flat button

pipe cleaner

twist-off bottle top

gold rickrack

thin gold cord, about 24 inches (61 centimeters) long

scissors

masking tape

aluminum foil

paper clip

white glue

Here is what you do:

1. Cut a piece of pipe cleaner 1 inch (2.5 centimeters) long. Bend the tip of one end of the pipe cleaner to the right and the tip of the other end to the left to form hooks.

Tape one hooked end of the pipe cleaner to the center of the button to make the base of the cup. Tape the other end to the center top of the bottle top to make the bowl of the cup.

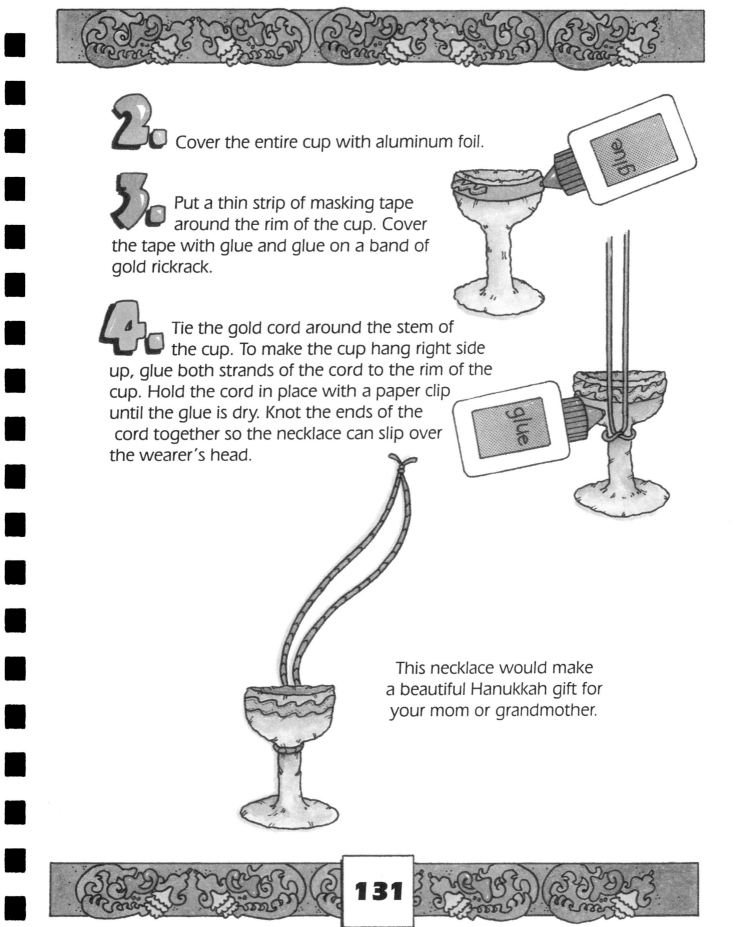

2. Cover the entire cup with aluminum foil.

3. Put a thin strip of masking tape around the rim of the cup. Cover the tape with glue and glue on a band of gold rickrack.

4. Tie the gold cord around the stem of the cup. To make the cup hang right side up, glue both strands of the cord to the rim of the cup. Hold the cord in place with a paper clip until the glue is dry. Knot the ends of the cord together so the necklace can slip over the wearer's head.

This necklace would make a beautiful Hanukkah gift for your mom or grandmother.

Maccabee Soldier

Soldiers led by Judah Maccabee recaptured
Jerusalem more than two thousand years ago.
Make your own Maccabee soldier.

Here is what you need:

piece of light-colored
12-inch by 18-inch
(30-centimeter by 46-
centimeter) fabric

permanent markers
in black and
other colors

white
glue

different
fabric trims

scissors

fiberfill

three clamp
clothespins

newspaper
to work on

Here is what you do:

1. Cut the fabric in half. Sketch
the outline of the Maccabee
soldier on one piece of the fabric
with a black permanent marker. (Be
sure to put newspaper down on the
table first because the marker might
soak through the fabric.) Use different colored markers to draw a face
and hair and clothes for the solider.
Glue fabric trim to the clothing.

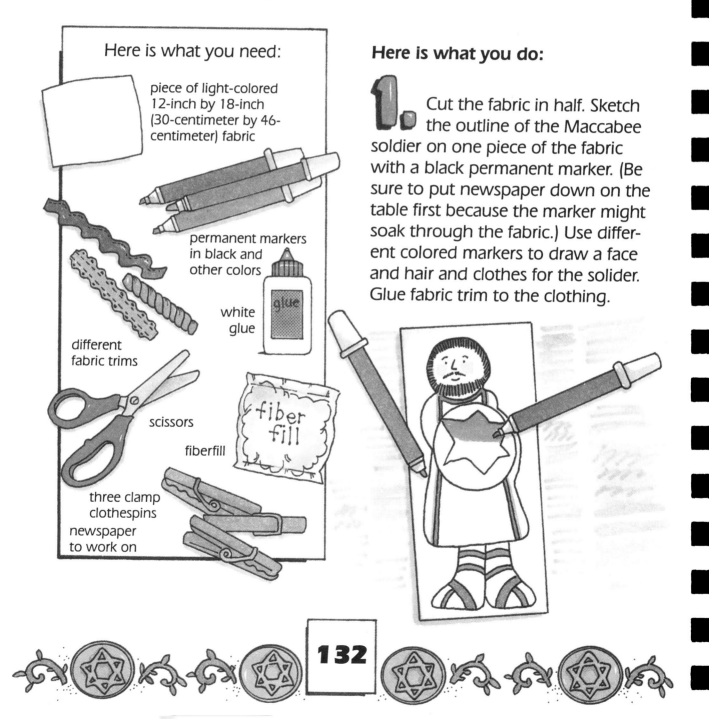

2. Turn the fabric over. You should be able to see the outline of the drawing on the other side. Put glue along the outline on this side, leaving about 3 inches (7.5 centimeters) of the drawing unglued at the bottom so you can put the stuffing in. Set the glued fabric on the other piece of fabric and let it dry.

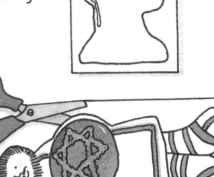

3. Carefully cut the soldier out around the outside of the glued edges. Stuff the doll with fiberfill and then glue the bottom opening shut. Use clamping clothespins to hold the edges together until the glue dries.

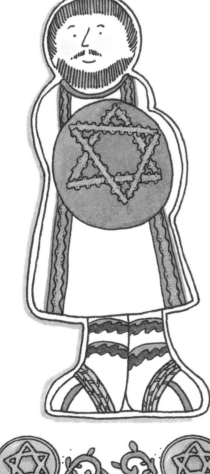

You might want to make a whole group of Maccabee soldiers.

Merry Christmas!

For Christians throughout the world Christmas is a celebration of great joy and hope because it is the birthday of Jesus, whom Christians believe to be the Son of God. Because the customs of the season are so popular and widely followed, many people celebrate the positive spirit of this holiday even though they may not embrace its specific religious beliefs.

The month of December is full of preparations for the big day on December 25. Wreaths may be hung on front doors, and trees may be decorated both indoors and out-doors. Special Christmas cookies and other foods are of-ten prepared, and presents are purchased or made and wrapped to be placed under the tree.

Whether celebrated as a religious holi-day, as a traditional holiday, or as both, Christmas can be a wonderful, exciting, and busy time for both young and old.

Three Kings Banner

Three wise men came to visit the Baby Jesus, bringing Him gifts of gold, frankincense, and myrrh.

Here is what you need:

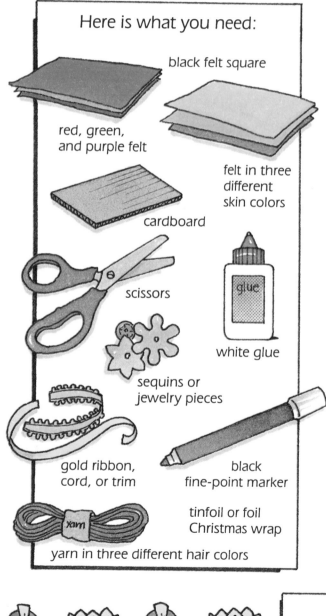

black felt square

red, green, and purple felt

felt in three different skin colors

cardboard

scissors

white glue

sequins or jewelry pieces

gold ribbon, cord, or trim

black fine-point marker

tinfoil or foil Christmas wrap

yarn in three different hair colors

Here is what you do:

1. Cut tall triangles from red, green, and purple felt to make the bodies of the three kings. Cut a head for each king from felt of a different skin shade. Arrange them on the black felt with the triangles slightly overlapping each other.

2. Draw a face on each king with a black marker. Cut up bits of yarn for the hair and beards, and glue them in place.

3. Cut crowns from foil and glue one on each king. Glue a jewel or cluster of sequins on the front of each king for a gift. You can also decorate their crowns and robes with gold ribbon, cord, trim, and sequins.

4. Cut a 1-inch (2.5-centimeter) strip of cardboard as long as the top of your banner. Cover both sides of the cardboard with glue and fold the top of the banner back over it to keep the banner stiff when you hang it.

Tuck the end of some gold cord or ribbon under the glue flap at each end of the banner and let the glue dry.

Flying Angel

Angels told of the birth of the Baby Jesus.

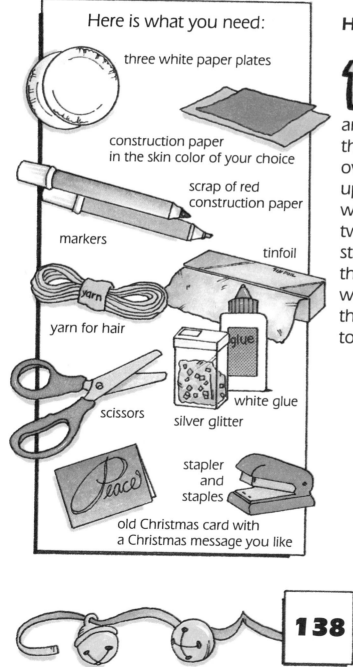

Here is what you need:

three white paper plates

construction paper
in the skin color of your choice

scrap of red
construction paper

markers

tinfoil

yarn for hair

white glue

scissors

silver glitter

stapler
and
staples

old Christmas card with
a Christmas message you like

Here is what you do:

1. Stack the three paper plates so that the rims are layered to one side and staple them together. Turn the plates over and cut from the layered rims up to a point on each side. This will make the angel dress. Cut two sleeves from the scraps and staple one to each side so that they are hanging down. Cut wings from the scraps and wrap them in tinfoil. Staple them to the top back of the angel.

2. Cut hands, feet, and a head for the angel from construction paper. Draw a face on the angel's head with markers. Cut heart-shaped cheeks from red paper and glue them in place. Cut bits of yarn for hair and glue them on. Squeeze a strip of tinfoil into the shape of a halo and glue it to the top of the angel's head. Glue the hands and feet in place.

3. Decorate the angel's dress with silver glitter. Cut a Christmas message from an old Christmas card and glue it between the angel's hands.

hands   feet

Peace

Jar Candleholder

Candles at Christmas represent the light brought into the world by the birth of the Baby Jesus.

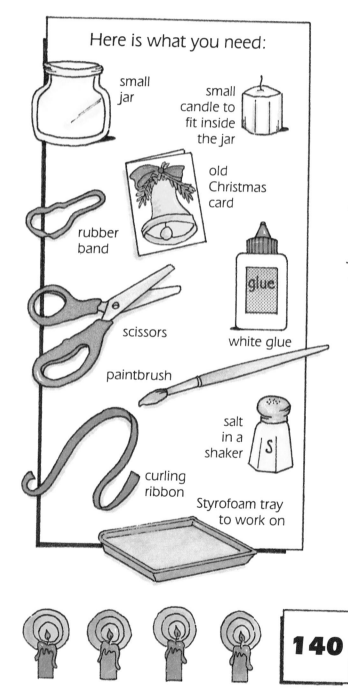

Here is what you need:

small jar

small candle to fit inside the jar

old Christmas card

rubber band

scissors

white glue

paintbrush

salt in a shaker

curling ribbon

Styrofoam tray to work on

Here is what you do:

1. Cut out a pretty picture from an old Christmas card; it should be small enough to fit on the side of the jar. Cover the back of the picture with glue, and glue it on the jar. Put a rubber band around the jar to hold the picture in place until the glue dries.

2. Remove the rubber band. Using a paintbrush, cover the outside of the jar and the picture with glue. Hold the jar over the Styrofoam tray and sprinkle salt over all of it to make the jar glisten. Let the jar dry on the tray.

3. Tie a piece of curling ribbon around the rim of the jar and curl the ends. Put the candle inside.

Jar candleholders make very nice Christmas presents.

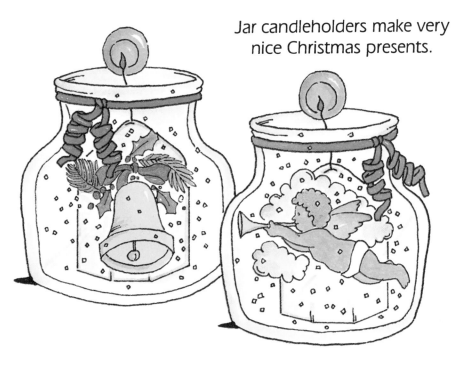

Christmas Story Pieces

The story of the birth of Baby Jesus is loved by all Christians, young and old, and is at the very center of the Christmas celebration. You can enact the story over and over again with this project.

Here is what you need:

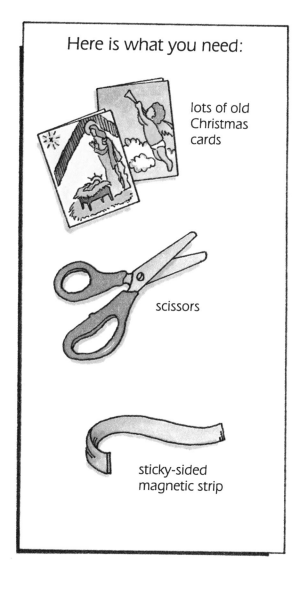

lots of old Christmas cards

scissors

sticky-sided magnetic strip

Here is what you do:

1. Look through old Christmas cards to find nice, large pictures of all the people and animals that were part of the Christmas story. You will need pictures of Mary and Joseph and the Baby Jesus, plus the shepherds, angels, wise men, sheep, camels, and whatever other animals you would like to include.

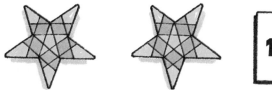

2. Cut carefully around each picture and stick a small piece of magnet on its back. You can arrange and play with your pictures on a refrigerator door or a cookie sheet.

Glitter and Sugar Ornament

Make lots of pretty ornaments to decorate your Christmas tree.

Here is what you need:

bowl

measuring cup

water

sugar

teaspoon

white glue

glitter in any color but clear

cookie cutters with backs

scissors

blue yarn

Here is what you do:

1. Pour 1/2 cup (about 120 milliliters) of sugar into a bowl. Add 1 teaspoon (about 5 milliliters) of glitter and mix well. Add 1 teaspoon (5 milliliters) of water and mix until the sugar is evenly moist.

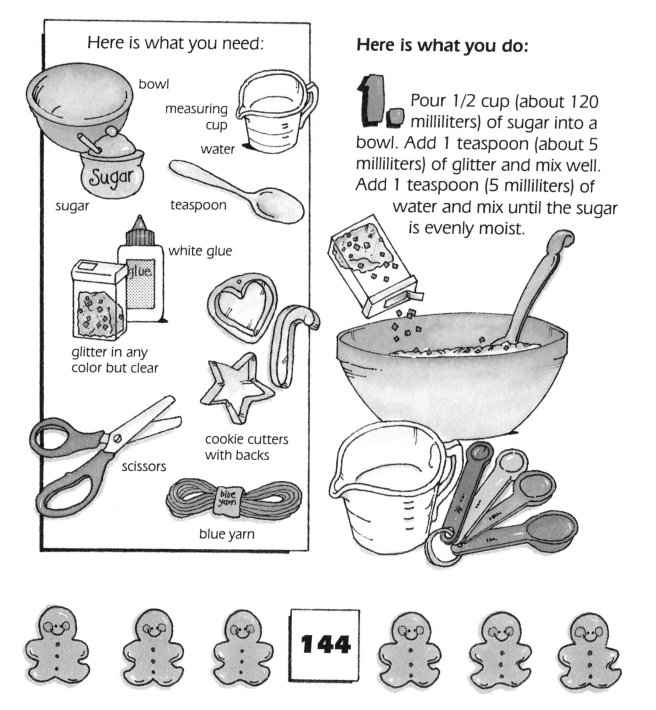

 2. Press the sugar into the cookie cutter, and then tap the ornament gently onto a plate. You should have enough sugar to make about four ornaments. Let them dry hard overnight.

3. When they are completely dry, glue a loop of yarn to the back of each one for a hanger.

Matchbox Present Ornament

At Christmastime, people exchange presents. Here is a present that goes on the tree instead of under it.

Here is what you need:

small matchbox

Christmas wrap with a small pattern

thin ribbon to match the wrapping paper

cellophane tape

scissors

yarn that matches the wrapping paper

Here is what you do:

1. Wrap the matchbox just as you would a present. Tie the ribbon around the tiny package and tie a bow.

2. Slip a piece of yarn under the ribbon and tie the two ends together to make a hanger.

Make lots of different package ornaments for your tree.

Rice Wreath Ornament

This tiny wreath hangs on the Christmas tree.

Here is what you need:

uncooked white rice

green food coloring

white glue

small margarine tub with a lid

spoon for mixing

measuring cup

scissors

red construction paper

red yarn

hole punch

hairpin

Here is what you do:

1. Pour three drops of green food coloring into 1/4 cup (60 milliliters) of glue and mix until the glue is evenly colored. Pour 1/2 cup (about 120 milliliters) of rice into the margarine tub, add the glue, and mix until the rice is completely coated with the green glue.

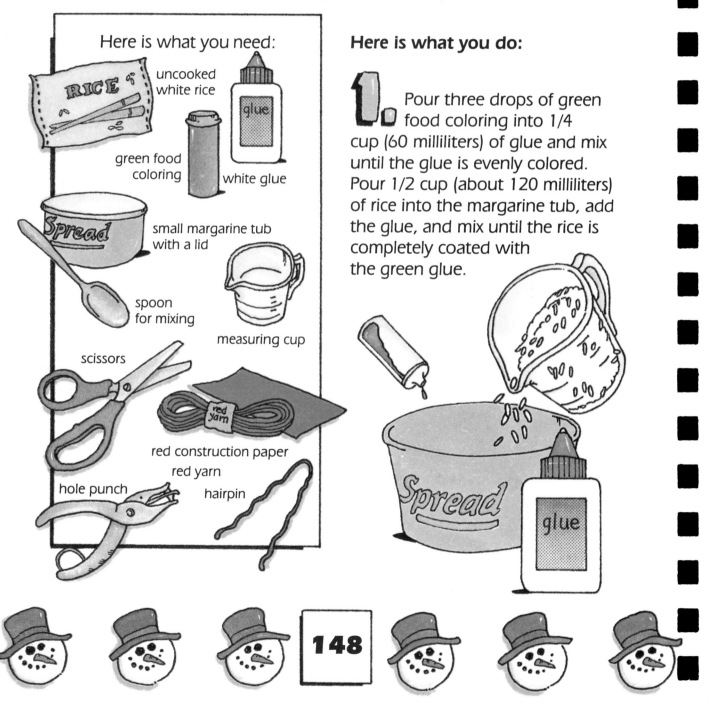

2. Spoon the rice mixture onto the margarine tub lid and shape it into a wreath. Push a hairpin into the edge of the wreath for a hanger and let the wreath dry overnight.

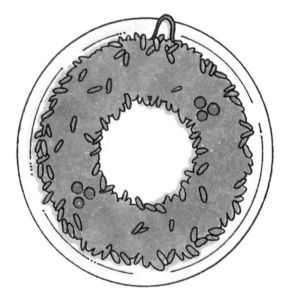

3. With a hole punch, punch berries from red construction paper and glue them on the wreath. Tie a yarn bow and glue it to the top of the wreath.

Santa Door Decoration

Children wait for Santa Claus to bring them presents to open on Christmas morning.

Here is what you need:

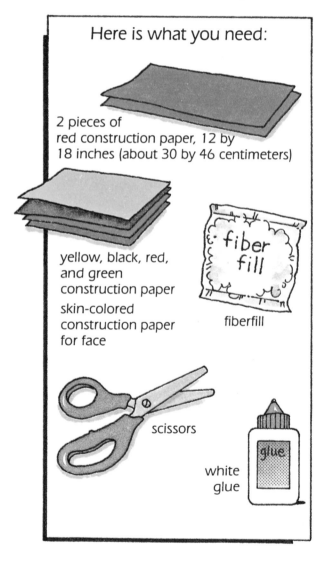

2 pieces of
red construction paper, 12 by
18 inches (about 30 by 46 centimeters)

yellow, black, red,
and green
construction paper

skin-colored
construction paper
for face

fiberfill

scissors

white
glue

Here is what you do:

1. Cut the two large sheets of red construction paper in half lengthwise. Glue two of the strips together at the top to form two legs. Glue another strip across the top of the legs to form arms.

2. Cut boots from black paper and mittens from green paper and glue them in place. Cut a face from skin-colored paper and glue it at the top of the body. Cut and glue on a red triangle hat and a black belt with a yellow buckle.

3. Glue fiberfill at the cuffs of the suit and on the rim and at the point of the hat. Glue a big fiberfill beard on the face.

4. Cut eyes from black paper and a nose and cheeks from red paper and glue them on for a face.

This Santa looks great holding a strip of ribbon, tiny lights, or a garland. Just tape an end of the ribbon, lights, or garland to each of the mittens.

Santa Claus Mask

Would you like to be Santa Claus?

Here is what you need:

paper plate

red and pink construction paper

fiber fill

fiberfill

scissors

white glue

stapler

Here is what you do:

1. Cut the center out of the paper plate and save the rim. Cut out a red triangle hat from the construction paper and glue it to the top of the rim. Glue a fiberfill ball at the point of the hat and a strip of fiberfill along the bottom of the hat.

2. Glue fiberfill all around the rim of the plate to make Santa's beard. Cut out pink cheeks and a red nose and glue them in place.

3. Staple the ends of a strip of red paper to each side of the back of the mask so that the strip forms a band to hold the mask in place.

What would you do if you were Santa Claus?

Stocking Game

Children hang up their stockings on Christmas Eve, hoping that Santa Claus will fill them with surprises. This stocking is one you try to fill yourself.

Here is what you need:

long sock

tall cardboard potato chip can

scissors

cotton balls or fiberfill for stuffing

white glue

hole punch

18-inch (46-centimeter) piece of red yarn

small toy

drinking glass that fits only part of the way into the can

Here is what you do:

1. Stuff the foot of the sock, leaving the heel portion empty. Push the can into the sock so that the bottom of the can fills the heel portion of the foot. Pull the sock up over the can as far as it will go and trim the top of the sock so that about 1 1/2 inches (about 4 centimeters) of it extends over the top of the can.

2. Rub glue around the inside rim of the can and fold the extra sock material over the rim to the inside of the can. Slide the drinking glass into the top of the can to hold the sock in place until the glue dries, then remove the glass.

3. Punch a hole in the top of the can. Tie one end of the yarn through the hole. Tie a small toy to the other end of the yarn.

The object of the game is to hold the bottom of the can and try to flip the toy into the stocking. You can make the game harder by using a longer string and easier by using a shorter string. You might also want to tie on more than one toy to try to flip into the sock.

Triangle Elf Ornament

Stories say that elves help Santa Claus make all those toys for good boys and girls.

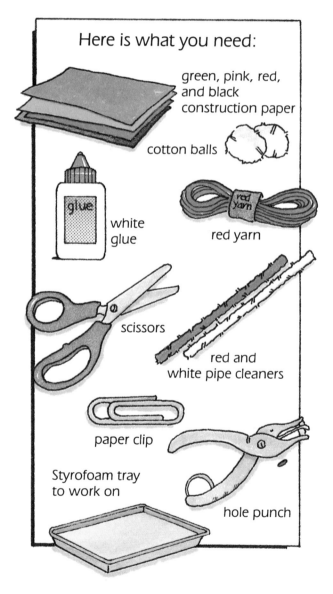

Here is what you need:

green, pink, red, and black construction paper

cotton balls

white glue

red yarn

scissors

red and white pipe cleaners

paper clip

Styrofoam tray to work on

hole punch

Here is what you do:

1. Cut two identical triangles from green paper with 4-inch (10-centimeter) bases and 6-inch (15-centimeter) sides. Cut two green rectangles for arms. Cut a head and hands from pink paper and boots from black paper.

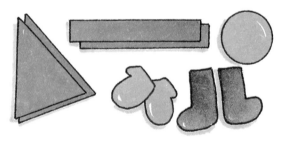

2. Put glue all over one triangle. Put the tops of the boots in the glue at the bottom of the triangle. Glue the end of an arm about halfway down on each side of the triangle and glue a hand

156

to the end of each arm. Cover the first triangle with the second one.

3. Glue the head about 2 inches (5 centimeters) down from the point of the triangle. Glue cotton across the top of the head, and glue a fluffed-out cotton ball on the face for a beard. Punch out eyes from black paper and cheeks and a nose from red paper and glue them in place.

4. Glue a piece of red yarn along the bottom of the triangle to trim the coat. Knot two short pieces of yarn and glue them to the front of the hat to form a tassel. Punch a hole in the top of the hat. String a long piece of yarn through the hole and tie the ends to make a hanger.

5. Twist two 4-inch (10-centimeter) pieces of pipe cleaner together to make a candy cane. Tie a yarn bow around the candy cane. Fold the elf's arms around in front to hold the candy cane and glue them in place. Use a paper clip to hold the arms together until the glue is dry.

Hand Reindeer

Santa uses flying reindeer to pull his sleigh full of toys.

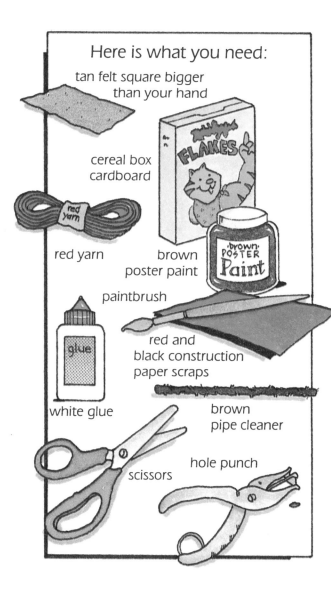

Here is what you need:

tan felt square bigger than your hand

cereal box cardboard

red yarn

brown poster paint

paintbrush

glue

red and black construction paper scraps

white glue

brown pipe cleaner

scissors

hole punch

Here is what you do:

1. Glue the tan felt square to the print side of the cardboard cut from a cereal box. Place heavy weights, like books, on both sides of the cardboard so it dries flat.

2. Paint the palm side of your hand brown. Spread your thumb and fingers out and carefully print your hand on the felt. Let the hand print dry.

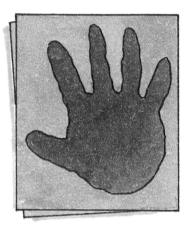

3. Cut the hand print out. The four fingers will be the reindeer legs and the thumb will be the head. Poke a hole at the base of the thumb and string a piece of brown pipe cleaner through for the antlers. Twist the two ends of the pipe cleaner around each other to hold them in place. Punch out an eye from black paper and a nose from red paper and glue them in place.

4. Tie a red yarn bow around the neck. Punch a hole at the top of the reindeer and string a piece of red yarn through it. Tie the two ends together to make a hanger.

Write a Christmas message on the back of your reindeer and give it to someone special for Christmas.

Reindeer Treat Bag

If it is foggy on Christmas Eve, Santa asks a red-nosed reindeer to use his shiny red nose to light the way.

Here is what you need:

piece of brown construction paper, 9 by 12 inches (23 by 30 centimeters)

white, black, and red paper scraps

white glue

stapler

cellophane tape

scissors

red ball lollipop

two candy canes

clear plastic wrap

Christmas-colored tissue paper

Here is what you do:

1. Wrap the sheet of brown construction paper around itself lengthwise and form a cone. Staple the cone in place. Fold down the corners on each side at the top to form reindeer ears.

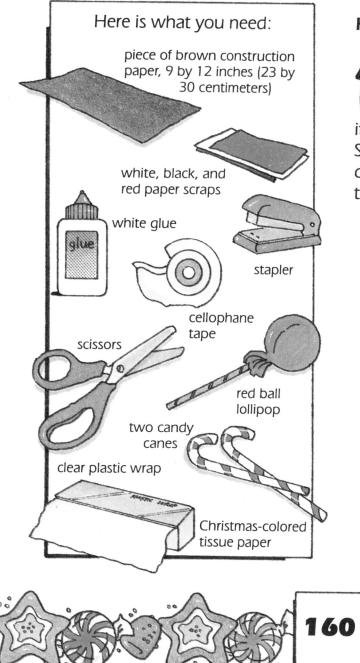

2. Cut eyes from white and black paper and glue them in place. Cut a handle from red paper and staple it across the top.

3. Unwrap the red lollipop and wrap it in clear plastic wrap to keep it clean. Slide the stick up into the hole at the point of the cone and tape the stick inside the cone so that the red ball forms the nose. Tape a candy cane inside the cone above each ear so that the hooks stick out to form the reindeer antlers.

Line the treat bag with Christmas-colored tissue and fill it with goodies to give to someone on your list.

Country Christmas Gift Bags

Gift bags are a pretty and easy way to wrap small gifts.

Here is what you need:

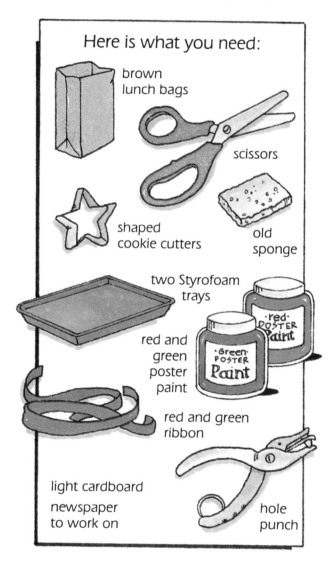

brown lunch bags

scissors

shaped cookie cutters

old sponge

two Styrofoam trays

red and green poster paint

red and green ribbon

light cardboard

newspaper to work on

hole punch

Here is what you do:

1. Make a stencil by tracing around a cookie cutter placed on light cardboard. Cut the shape out without cutting through the surrounding cardboard. Gingerbread boys, hearts, stars, and Christmas trees all work well for this project.

2. Pour some paint onto a Styrofoam tray and spread the paint around with a piece of sponge. Carefully place the cardboard stencil in the center of one

162

side of a flattened bag. Use the sponge to dab paint in the cut-out portion of the stencil. The shape of the stencil will appear on the bag. Make several different bags using different shapes and different colors of paint. Let the bags dry, then stencil the other sides.

Merry Christmas!

3. Fold the top of each bag over and punch two holes below the fold. String some pretty Christmas ribbon through the holes and tie it in a bow above the stenciled shape in order to close the bag.

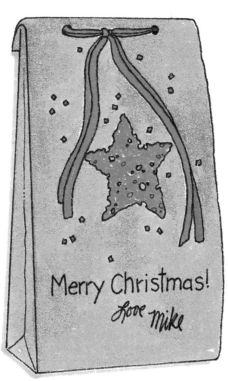

Merry Christmas! Love mike

If you wish, you can add details to your shapes using cut paper, sequins, or glitter.

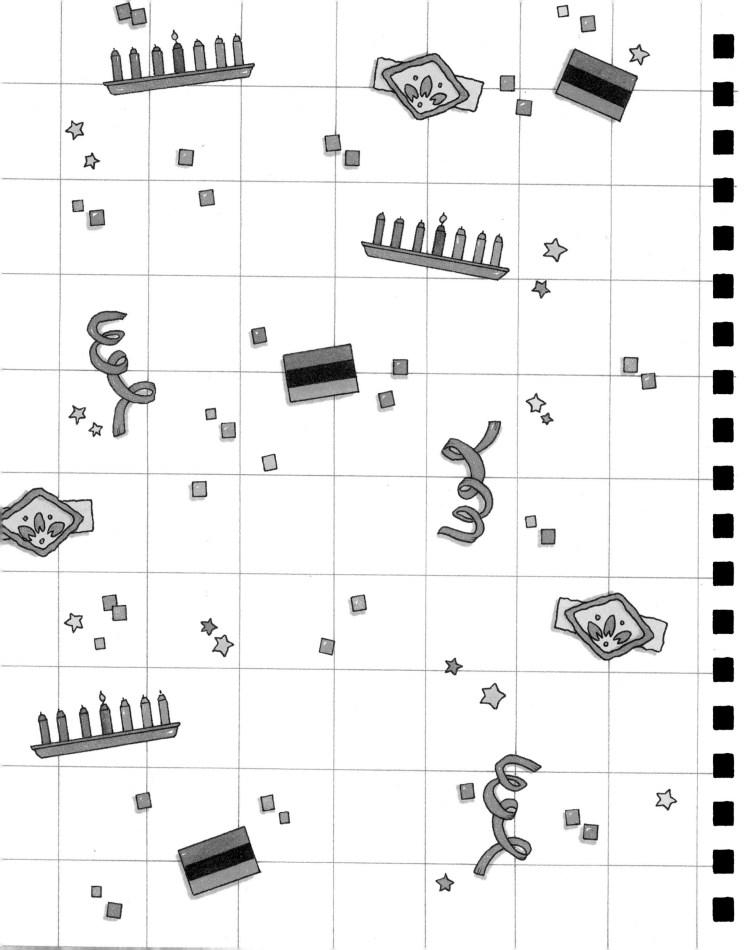

Celebrating Kwanzaa

Kwanzaa is a holiday celebrating the African roots of black Americans. It begins on December 26 and lasts for seven days. The colors of Kwanzaa are red, black, and green—the colors of the flag created by African-American leader Marcus Garvey in the early 1900s. Red represents the struggle for freedom. Black is for black people united. Green symbolizes the future of black people.

The African language of Swahili is used to name the symbols and words used at Kwanzaa time. The name "Kwanzaa" itself comes from a Swahili word for the first fruits of the harvest. The values expressed through this holiday are reflected in the *nguzo saba* (or seven principles) of Kwanzaa written by Dr. Maulana Karenga, a teacher who created this celebration in 1966.

Nguzo Saba
The Seven Principles of Kwanzaa

Umoja (Unity)   *Nia* (Purpose)
Kujichagulia (Self-Determination)
Ujima (Collective Work and Responsibility)
Ujamaa (Cooperative Economics)
Kuumba (Creativity)   *Imani* (Faith)

Light the Kwanzaa Candles....

Corn Necklace

Munhindi means corn. The corn represents the children of a family. Make your mom a necklace with one ear of corn for each child in your family.

Here is what you need:

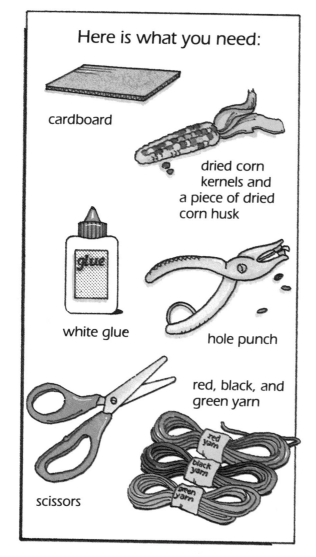

cardboard

dried corn kernels and a piece of dried corn husk

white glue

hole punch

scissors

red, black, and green yarn

Here is what you do:

1. Cut a corn shape from cardboard for each ear of corn on your necklace. Punch two holes in the top of each one and string them across strands of the three colors of yarn cut to form a necklace.

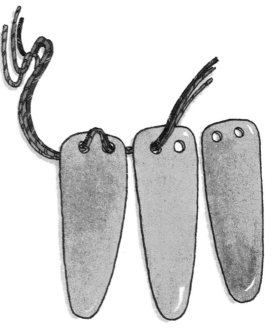

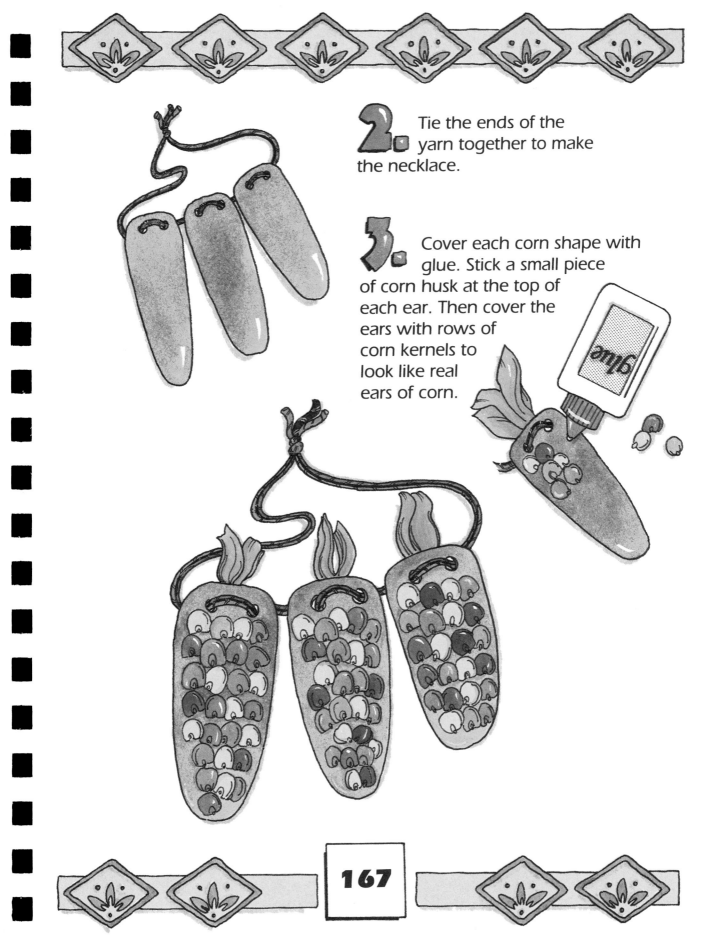

2. Tie the ends of the yarn together to make the necklace.

3. Cover each corn shape with glue. Stick a small piece of corn husk at the top of each ear. Then cover the ears with rows of corn kernels to look like real ears of corn.

glue

Kwanzaa
Candles Game

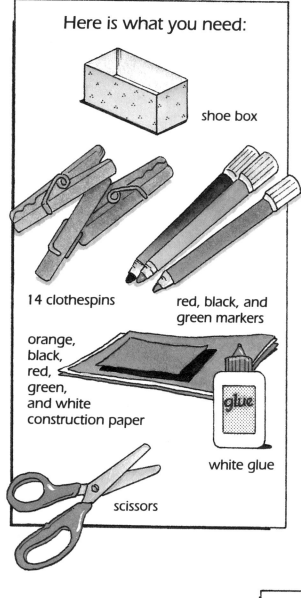

Here is what you need:

shoe box

14 clothespins

red, black, and green markers

orange, black, red, green, and white construction paper

white glue

scissors

Here is what you do:

1. You will need to make six red, six green, and two black candles from construction paper. Make them the height and width of the clothespins. Cut out 14 flame shapes from the orange paper and glue one to the top of each candle. Then glue one candle to each clothespin so that it can be clamped on the shoe box with the flame on top.

2. Cut 14 cards about 2 inches (5 centimeters) square from the white paper. Draw a black candle on two cards, a red candle on six cards, and a green candle on six cards.

Here is how to play the game:
This game is for two players. Give each player one black, three red, and three green candles. Put the cards face down in the shoe box. The players sit facing each other with the box between them. The object of the game is to see who can get all of their Kwanzaa candles lined up on the box first. The candles must be placed in the order they are lighted for each day of Kwanzaa. The black candle comes first (in the middle), then the red candles on the left, then the green candles on the right. Players alternate red and green until all seven candles are on the box. To get candles, players take turns drawing from

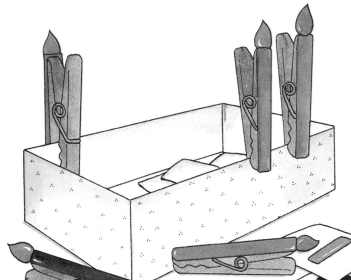

the cards in the box. If the player uses a card he or she takes it from the box, but if the card cannot be used, it is mixed back into the pile. Players may draw cards to see who goes first, with black being first.

Corn Print Wrapping Paper

Zawadi means gifts. The last day of Kwanzaa is a time for sharing gifts. Here are some ideas for wrapping and tagging your gifts.

Here is what you need:

newspaper to cover your work surface

ear of corn or corncob

white tissue paper

orange and yellow poster paint

two Styrofoam trays

Here is what you do:

1. Pour one color of paint into each tray.

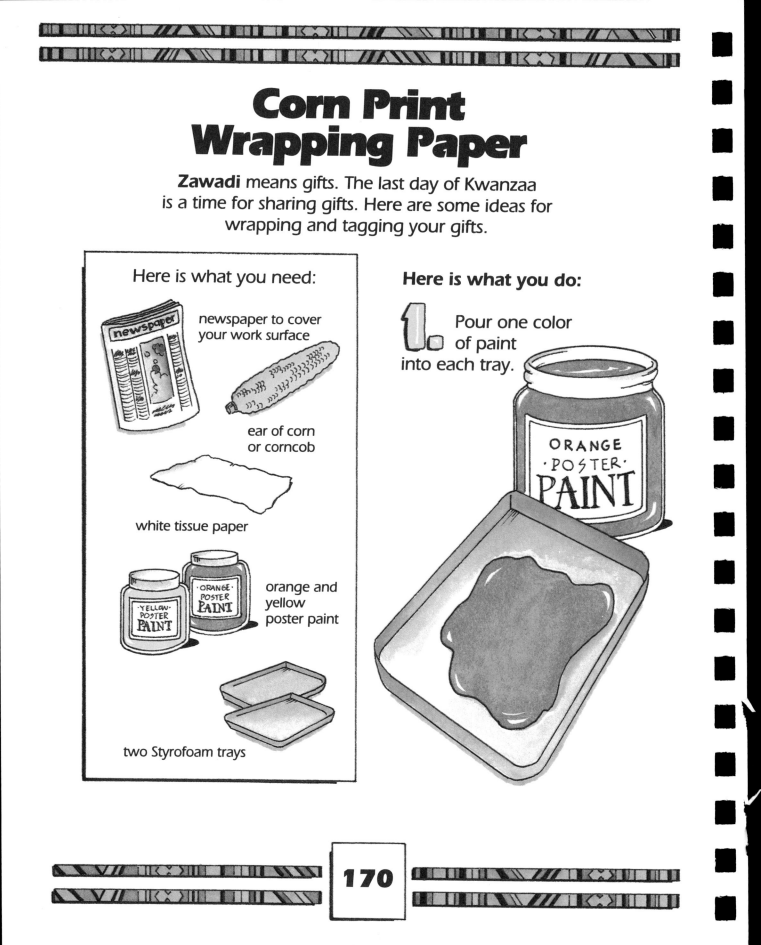

2. Roll the corn in the yellow paint first. Then roll it across the paper in several different directions to print the paper with the design of the corn.

3. Do the same with the orange paint. Let the tissue dry flat.

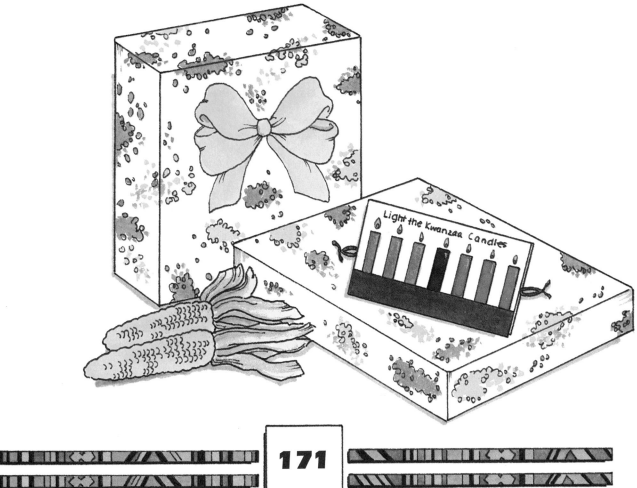

Kwanzaa Memory Book

Make a memory book for photographs and drawings of your Kwanzaa celebration. This book would make a nice Kwanzaa gift.

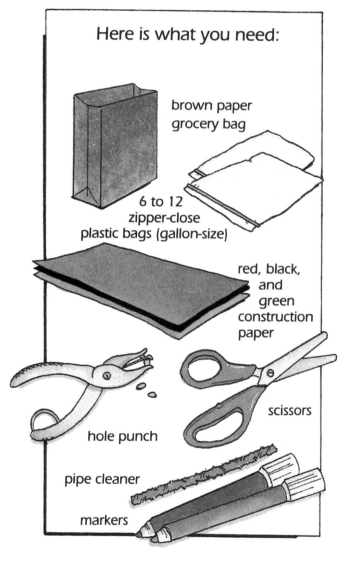

Here is what you need:

brown paper grocery bag

6 to 12 zipper-close plastic bags (gallon-size)

red, black, and green construction paper

hole punch

scissors

pipe cleaner

markers

Here is what you do:

1. The plastic bags will be the pages of your book. Stack them so that the bottoms of the bags are on your left. From the brown paper bag, cut a cover that folds around the plastic bags to form both the front and back of the book. (The cover should be a little larger than the pages.) Make sure all the pages are lined up inside the cover.

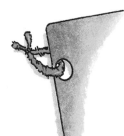

Then punch a hole near the top and the bottom of the fold. Use pieces of pipe cleaner strung through the holes, with the ends twisted together, to hold the book together.

2. Use markers to color a picture on the front of your memory book. Cut pieces of red, green, or black construction paper to fit inside each of the plastic pages of your book. Then you can tape photographs, drawings, and other small memories of your holiday celebration to the front and back of each construction paper sheet, and they will be protected by the plastic pages.

My Kwanzaa Memory Book

Kwanzaa Hug Card

Here is what you need:

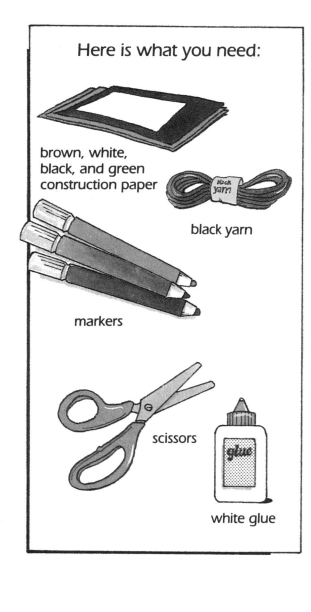

brown, white, black, and green construction paper

black yarn

markers

scissors

white glue

Here is what you do:

1. Cut a circle about the size of a dinner plate out of brown paper. Give the circle a face using paper cut-outs and markers. Glue on yarn hair.

2. Cut a strip of green paper 18 inches (46 centimeters) long and 4 inches (10 centimeters) wide for the arms. Glue the head to the top middle of the strip. Trace around your hands on brown paper and cut out the hand shapes. Glue one at the end of each arm. Fold the arms toward the middle so that the hands overlap slightly.

Here is a big Kwanzaa Hug for you! love-Jason

3. Open the arms up and write "Here is a big Kwanzaa hug for you" and sign your name. Close the arms and give the surprise hug to someone special.

Hug
love-Jason

About the author and illustrator

Twenty years as a teacher and director of nursery school programs have given Kathy Ross extensive experience in guiding young children through craft projects. Her craft projects have appeared in *Highlights* magazine, and she has also written numerous songs for young children. She is the author of the Holiday Crafts for Kids series, on which this book is based, as well as *Gifts to Make for Your Favorite Grownups*. She lives in Oneida, New York.

Sharon Lane Holm won awards for her work in advertising design before shifting her concentration to children's books. Her illustrations have since added zest to books for both the trade and educational markets. She lives in New Fairfield, Connecticut.